Frank Cioppa

D0948879

The Mind of the Maker

DOROTHY L. SAYERS

The Mind
of the Maker

GREENWOOD PRESS, PUBLISHERS
WESTPORT, CONNECTICUT

The Library of Congress cataloged this book as follows:

Sayers, Dorothy Leigh, 1893–1957.
    The mind of the Maker. Westport, Conn., Greenwood
Press [1970, °1941]
       xiv, 229 p. 23 cm.

1. Christianity—Philosophy.   I. Title.

BR100.S3 1970   201   72–106698
ISBN 0–8371–3372–6   MARC
Library of Congress   71 [4]

IN GLORIAM MAIOREM
SANCTI ATHANASII
QUI OPIFICIS AETERNI DIVINITATEM
CONTRA MUNDUM VINDICAVIT
ITEM
ECCLESIARUM BRITANNICARUM
PER DUCES SUOS CONTRA MUNDUM
OPERUM HUMANORUM SANCTITATEM
HODIE ASSERENTIUM

I propose to state the doctrine of the Trinity of God . . . in doing which, if I shall be led on to mention one or two points of detail, it must not be supposed, as some persons strangely mistake, as if such additional statements were intended for explanation, *whereas they leave the Great Mystery just as it was before, and are only useful as impressing on our mind* what *it is which the Catholic Church means to assert, and to make it a matter of real faith and apprehension, and not a mere assemblage of words.*

—JOHN HENRY NEWMAN: *Sermon on the Trinity*

In the case of man, that which he creates is more expressive of him than that which he begets. The image of the artist and the poet is imprinted more clearly on his works than on his children.

—NICHOLAS BERDYAEV: *The Destiny of Man*

PREFACE

THIS book is not an apology for Christianity, nor is it an expression of personal religious belief. It is a commentary, in the light of specialized knowledge, on a particular set of statements made in the Christian creeds and their claim to be statements of fact.

It is necessary to issue this caution, for the popular mind has grown so confused that it is no longer able to receive any statement of fact except as an expression of personal feeling. Some time ago, the present writer, pardonably irritated by a very prevalent ignorance concerning the essentials of Christian doctrine, published a brief article in which those essentials were plainly set down in words that a child could understand. Every clause was preceded by some such phrase as: "the Church maintains," "the Church teaches," "if the Church is right," and so forth. The only personal opinion expressed was that, though the doctrine might be false, it could not very well be called dull.

Every newspaper that reviewed this article accepted it without question as a profession of faith—some (Heaven knows why) called it "a courageous profession of faith," as though professing Christians in this country were liable to instant persecution. One review, syndicated throughout the Empire, called it "a personal confession of faith by a woman who feels sure she is right."

Now, what the writer believes or does not believe is of little importance one way or the other. What is of great and disastrous importance is the proved inability of supposedly educated persons to read. So far from expressing any personal belief or any claim to personal infallibility, the writer had simply offered a flat recapitulation of official doctrine, adding that nobody was obliged to believe it. There was not a single word or sentence from which a personal opinion could legitimately be deduced, and for all the article contained it might perfectly well have been written by a well-informed Zoroastrian.

It is common knowledge among school-teachers that a high percentage of examination failures results from "not reading the question." The candidate presumably applies his eyes to the paper, but his answer shows that he is incapable of discovering by that process what the question is. This means that he is not only slovenly-minded but, in all except the most superficial sense, illiterate. Teachers further complain that they have to spend a great deal of time and energy in teaching University students what questions to ask. This indicates that the young mind experiences great difficulty in disentangling the essence of a subject from its accidents; and it is disconcertingly evident, in discussions on the platform and in the press, that the majority of people never learn to overcome this difficulty. A third distressing phenomenon is the extreme unwillingness of the average questioner to listen to the answer—a phenomenon exhibited in exaggerated form by professional interviewers on the staffs of popular journals. It is a plain fact that ninety-nine interviews out of a hundred contain more or less subtle distortions of the answers given to questions, the questions being, moreover, in many cases, wrongly conceived for the purpose of eliciting the truth. The distortions are not confined to distortions of opinion but are frequently also distortions of fact, and not merely stupid misunderstandings at that, but deliberate falsifications. The journalist is, indeed, not interested in the facts. For this he is to some extent excusable, seeing that, even if he published the facts, his public would inevitably distort them in the reading. What is quite inexcusable is that when the victim of misrepresentation writes to protest and correct the statements attributed to him, his protest is often ignored and his correction suppressed. Nor has he any redress, since to misrepresent a man's statements is no offense, unless the misrepresentation happens to fall within the narrow limits of the law of libel. The Press and the Law are in this condition because the public do not care whether they are being told truth or not.

The education that we have so far succeeded in giving to the bulk of our citizens has produced a generation of mental slatterns. They are literate in the merely formal sense—that is, they are capable of putting the symbols C, A, T together to produce the word CAT. But they are not literate in the sense of deriving from those letters any clear mental concept of the animal. Literacy in the formal sense is dangerous, since it lays the mind open to receive any mischievous nonsense about cats that an irresponsible writer may choose to print—nonsense which could never have entered the heads of plain illiterates who were familiar with an actual cat, even if unable to spell its name. And particularly in the matter of Christian doctrine, a great part of the nation subsists in an ignorance more barbarous than that of the dark ages, owing to this slatternly habit of illiterate reading. Words are understood in a wholly mistaken sense, statements of fact and opinion are misread and distorted in repetition, arguments founded in misapprehension are accepted without examination, expressions of individual preference are construed as oecumenical doctrine, disciplinary regulations founded on consent are confused with claims to interpret universal law, and vice versa; with the result that the logical and historical structure of Christian philosophy is transformed in the popular mind to a confused jumble of mythological and pathological absurdity.

It is for this reason that I have prefixed to this brief study of the creative mind an introductory chapter in which I have tried to make clear the difference between fact and opinion, and between the so-called "laws" based on fact and opinion respectively.

In the creeds of Christendom, we are confronted with a set of documents which purport to be, not expressions of opinion but statements of fact. Some of these statements are historical, and with these the present book is not concerned. Others are theological—which means that they claim to be statements of fact about the nature of God and the universe; and with a limited number of these I propose to deal.

The selected statements are those which aim at defining the nature of God, conceived in His capacity as Creator. They were originally drawn up as defenses against heresy—that is, specifically to safeguard the facts against opinions which were felt to be distortions of fact. It will not do to regard them as the product of irresponsible speculation, spinning fancies for itself in a vacuum. That is the reverse of the historical fact about them. They would never have been drawn up at all but for the urgent practical necessity of finding a formula to define experienced truth under pressure of misapprehension and criticism.

The point I shall endeavor to establish is that these statements about God the Creator are not, as is usually supposed, a set of arbitrary mystifications irrelevant to human life and thought. On the contrary, whether or not they are true about God, they are, when examined in the light of direct experience, seen to be plain witness of truth about the nature of the creative mind as such and as we know it. So far as they are applicable to man, they embody a very exact description of the human mind while engaged in an act of creative imagination. Whether this goes to prove that man is made in the image of God, or merely that God has been made in the image of man, is an argument that I shall not pursue, since the answer to that question depends upon those historical statements which lie outside my terms of reference. The Christian affirmation is, however, that the Trinitarian structure which can be shown to exist in the mind of man and in all his works is, in fact, the integral structure of the universe, and corresponds, not by pictorial imagery but by a necessary uniformity of substance, with the nature of God, in Whom all that is exists.

This, I repeat, is the Christian affirmation. It is not my invention, and its truth or falsehood cannot be affected by any opinions of mine. I shall try only to demonstrate that the statements made in the Creeds about the Mind of the Divine Maker represent, so far as I am able to check them by my experience, true statements about the mind of the human maker. *If* the statements are theologically true, then the inference to be drawn about the present social and educational system is important, and perhaps alarming; but I have expressed no personal opinion about their theological truth or otherwise; I am not writing "as a Christian," but as [1] a professional writer. Nobody, I hope, will be so illiterate as to assert that, in pointing out this plain fact, I am disclaiming belief in Christianity. This book proves nothing either way about my religious opinions, for the very sufficient reason that they are not so much as mentioned.

[1] If one must use this curious expression. The theory that what writes is not the self but some aspect of the self is popular in these days. It assists pigeon-holing. It is, of course, heretical—a form of Sabellianism,[2] no doubt. Even so, it is very loosely used. "Mr. Jones writes as a coal-miner" usually means that the critic knows Mr. Jones to be a miner, and takes it for granted that he understands mining. But "Mr. Smith writes as a Christian" may mean only that the critic perceives Mr. Smith to have some understanding of Christianity, and takes it for granted that he is a Christian. "This fact [*that I had many Christian friends*]," says Mr. Herbert Read, plaintively, "together with my intellectual interest in religion, and at one time my frequent reference to scholasticism, has often led to the assumption that I was at least in sympathy with the Catholic Church, and perhaps a neo-Thomist" (*Annals of Innocence and Experience*). Naturally; what else could he expect?

[2] Sabellius was a theologian of the third century, who maintained that God was not at one and the same time, Father, Son, and Spirit, but assumed these manifestations consecutively. His heresy died out in the fourth century.—EDITOR'S NOTE.

CONTENTS

I

THE "LAWS" OF NATURE AND OPINION

A stranger to our University, observing that undergraduates were inside their colleges before midnight, might believe that he had discovered a law of human nature—that there is something in the nature of the undergraduate which impels him to seek the protection of the college walls before the stroke of twelve. We must undeceive him, and point out that the law has a quite different source—the College authorities. Should he conclude then that the law is altogether independent of undergraduate nature? Not necessarily. Careful research would reveal that the law depends on considerable antecedent experience of undergraduate nature. We cannot say that the twelve o'clock rule is not based on undergraduate nature; but it is not based on it in in the way the stranger assumed. —SIR ARTHUR EDDINGTON: *The Philosophy of Physical Science*

THE "LAWS" OF NATURE AND OPINION

THE word "law" is currently used in two quite distinct meanings. It may describe an arbitrary regulation made by human consent in particular circumstances for a particular purpose, and capable of being promulgated, enforced, suspended, altered, or rescinded without interference with the general scheme of the universe. In this sense we may talk of Roman "Law," the "laws" of civilized warfare, or the "laws" of cricket. Such laws frequently prescribe that certain events shall follow upon certain others; but the second event is not a *necessary* consequence of the first: the connection between the two is purely formal. Thus, if the ball (correctly bowled) hits the wicket, the batsman is "out." There is, however, no inevitable connection between the impact of the ball upon three wooden stumps and the progress of a human body from a patch of mown grass to a pavilion. The two events are readily separable in theory. If the M.C.C.[1] chose to alter the "law," they could do so immediately, by merely saying so, and no cataclysm of nature would be involved. The l.b.w.[2] rule has, in fact, been altered within living memory, and not merely the universe, but even the game, has survived the altera-

[1] Marylebone Cricket Club (the world's leading club devoted to the game).—EDITOR'S NOTE.
[2] L. B. W. means "leg before the wicket," and indicates one of the nine ways in which the "striker" or batsman can be put out.—EDITOR'S NOTE.

tion. Similarly, if a twentieth-century Englishman mar-
ries two wives at once, he goes to prison—but only if
he is found out; there is no necessary causal connection
between over-indulgence in matrimony and curtailment
of personal liberty (in the formal sense, that is; in another, one may say that to marry even one wife is to
renounce one's freedom); in Mohammedan countries
any number of wives up to four is, or was, held to be
both lawful and morally right. And in warfare, the restrictions forbidding the use of poison-gas and the
indiscriminate sowing of mines must, unfortunately,
be regarded rather as pious aspirations than as
"laws" entailing consequences even of a conventional
kind.

In its other use, the word "law" is employed to desig-
nate a generalized statement of observed fact of one sort
or another. Most of the so-called "laws of nature" are
of this kind: "If you hold your finger in the fire it will
be burnt"; "if you vary the distance between an object
and a source of light, the intensity of the light at the
surface of the object will vary inversely as the square of
the distance." Such "laws" as these cannot be promulgated, altered, suspended, or broken at will; they are
not "laws" at all, in the sense that the laws of cricket
or the laws of the realm are "laws"; they are statements
of observed facts inherent in the nature of the universe.
Anybody can enact that murder shall not be punishable
by death; nobody can enact that the swallowing of a
tumblerful of prussic acid shall not be punishable by
death. In the former case, the connection between the
two events is legal—that is, arbitrary; in the latter, it is a

true causal connection, and the second event is a necessary consequence of the first.[3]

The word "law" is applied also to statements of observed fact of a rather different kind. It is used, for example, as a handy expression to sum up a general tendency, in cases where a given effect usually, though not necessarily, follows a given cause. Thus the Mendelian "law" of inheritance expresses the observed fact that the mating of, for example, black with white will—taking it by and large—produce black, white and mulatto offspring in a certain numerical proportion,[4] though not necessarily with arithmetical exactitude in any one case. The same word is also used to express a *tendency* which

[3] The conclusions reached by the physicists seem to show that the "laws" governing the behavior of inanimate matter can be reduced to one "law," namely: that there is no "law" or code in the arbitrary sense; that matter "shakes down at random," "goes anyhow," "does as it likes," "does whatever is statistically most probable." This is only another way of saying that the "laws" of the physical universe are observations of fact; we say that matter is bound to behave as it does because that is the way we see that matter behaves. Consequently, we cannot use the "laws" of physics to construct a hypothetical universe of a different physical kind; those "laws" are observations of fact about *this* universe, so that, according to them, no other kind of physical universe is possible. Animate nature, on the other hand, while obeying the "law" of randomness, appears to be characterized by an additional set of "laws," including, among other things, the properties of using physical randomness for the construction of purposive order, and of promulgating arbitrary codes to regulate its own behavior. See Reginald O. Kapp: *Science versus Materialism*, Section II, "Double Determinateness."

[4] Handily summed up for mnemonic convenience in the famous Limerick:

> There was a young lady called Starkie,
> Who had an affair with a darkie;
> The result of her sins
> Was quadruplets, not twins,
> One black and one white and two khaki.

has been observed to occur, as a historic fact, over speci-
fied periods. For instance, the philologist Jakob Grimm
observed that certain phonetic changes took place in particular consonants during the development of the Teu-
tonic languages from the primitive roots which they
share with Greek and Sanskrit, and the summary of
his observations is known as "Grimm's Law." "Thus
Grimm's Law may be defined as the *statement of certain*
phonetic *facts* which happen invariably unless they are
interfered with by other facts." [5] A "law" of this kind
is, therefore, very like a "law of nature." An apple, we
may say, when it leaves the tree, will invariably fall to
the ground unless there is some interference with the law
—unless, for example, the hand of Isaac Newton arrests
it in mid-fall. There is, however, this difference: that
we can readily conceive of a universe in which Grimm's
Law did not function; the world would remain substantially the same world if Sanskrit *t*, instead of being represented by *d* in Old High German, had been represented by something different; whereas a world in which
apples did not fall would be very unlike the world in
which we live. Grimm's "law" is, in short, a statement
of historical fact, whereas the "laws" of nature are statements of physical fact: the one expresses what *has* in
fact happened; the others, what *does* in fact happen. But
both are statements of observed fact about the nature of
the universe. Certain things are observed to occur, and
their occurrence does not depend upon human consent
or opinion. The village that voted the earth was flat
doubtless modified its own behavior and its system of

[5] *Chambers' Encyclopaedia*: Art. Grimm (Jakob).

physics accordingly, but its vote did not in any way modify the shape of the earth. That remains what it is, whether human beings agree or disagree about it, or even if they never discuss it or take notice of it at all. And if the earth's shape entails consequences for humanity, those consequences will continue to occur, whether humanity likes it or not, in conformity with the laws of nature.

The vote of the M.C.C. about cricket, on the other hand, does not merely alter a set of theories about cricket; it alters the game. That is because cricket is a human invention, whose laws depend for their existence and validity upon human consent and human opinion. There would be no laws and no cricket unless the M.C.C. were in substantial agreement about what sort of thing cricket ought to be—if, for example, one party thought of it as a species of steeplechase, while another considered it to be something in the nature of a ritual dance. Its laws, being based upon a consensus of opinion, can be enforced by the same means; a player who deliberately disregards them will not be invited to play again, since opinion—which made the laws—will unite to punish the law-breaker. Arbitrary law is, therefore, possessed of valid authority provided it observes two conditions:—

The first condition is that public opinion shall strongly endorse the law. This is understandable, since opinion *is* the authority. An arbitrary law unsupported by a consensus of opinion will not be properly enforced and will in the end fall into disrepute and have to be rescinded or altered. This happened to the Prohibition Laws in America. It is happening today to the laws of civilized warfare, because German opinion refuses to acknowledge them, and the consensus of world opinion is not sufficiently powerful to enforce them against German consent. We express the situation very accurately when we say that Germany is "not playing the game"—admitting by that phrase that the "laws" of combat are arbitrary, like the "laws" of a game, and have no validity except in a general consensus of opinion.

The second condition is, of course, that the arbitrary law shall not run counter to the law of nature. If it does, it not only will not, it cannot be enforced. Thus, if the M.C.C. were to agree, in a thoughtless moment, that the ball must be so hit by the batsman that it should never come down to earth again, cricket would become an impossibility. A vivid sense of reality usually restrains sports committees from promulgating laws of this kind; other legislators occasionally lack this salutary realism. When the laws regulating human society are so formed as to come into collision with the nature of things, and in particular with the fundamental realities of human nature, they will end by producing an impossible situation which, unless the laws are altered, will issue in such catastrophes as war, pestilence and famine. Catastrophes thus caused are the execution of universal law upon arbitrary enactments which contravene the facts; they are thus properly called by theologians, judgments of God.

Much confusion is caused in human affairs by the use of the same word "law" to describe these two very different things: an arbitrary code of behavior based on a consensus of human opinion and a statement of unalterable fact about the nature of the universe.[6] The confu-

6 cf. E. H. Carr: *The Twenty Years' Crisis*, Chap. X.

sion is at its worst when we come to talk about the "moral law." Professor Macmurray,[7] for example, contrasting the moral law with the law of nature, says, "The essence of . . . a mechanical morality will be the idea that goodness consists in obedience to a moral law. Such a morality is false, because it destroys human spontaneity . . . by subjecting it to an external authority. . . . It is only matter that can be free in obeying laws." What he is doing here is to use the words "law" and "laws" in two different senses. When he speaks of the "laws" governing the behavior of matter, he means statements of observed fact about the nature of the material universe; when he speaks of a moral "law," he means the arbitrary code of behavior established by human opinion.

There is a universal moral law, as distinct from a moral code, which consists of certain statements of fact about the nature of man; and by behaving in conformity with which, man enjoys his true freedom. This is what the Christian Church calls "the natural law." [8] The more closely the moral code agrees with the natural law, the more it makes for freedom in human behavior; the more widely it departs from the natural law, the more it tends to enslave mankind and to produce the catastrophes called "judgments of God."

The universal moral *law* (or natural law of humanity) is discoverable, like any other law of nature, by experience. It cannot be promulgated, it can only be

[7] *Freedom in the Modern World.*
[8] "The natural law may be described briefly as a force working in history which tends to keep human beings human."—J. V. Langmead Casserley: *The Fate of Modern Culture.*

ascertained, because it is a question not of opinion but of fact. When it has been ascertained, a moral *code* can be drawn up to direct human behavior and prevent men, as far as possible, from doing violence to their own nature. No code is necessary to control the behavior of matter, since matter is apparently not tempted to contradict its own nature, but obeys the law of its being in perfect freedom. Man, however, does continually suffer this temptation and frequently yields to it. This contradiction within his own nature is peculiar to man, and is called by the Church "sinfulness"; other psychologists have other names for it.

The moral *code* depends for its validity upon a consensus of human opinion about what man's nature really is, and what it ought to be, when freed from this mysterious self-contradiction and enabled to run true to itself. If there is no agreement about these things, then it is useless to talk of enforcing the moral code. It is idle to complain that a society is infringing a moral code intended to make people behave like St. Francis of Assisi if the society retorts that it does not wish to behave like St. Francis, and considers it more natural and right to behave like the Emperor Caligula. When there is a genuine conflict of opinion, it is necessary to go behind the moral code and appeal to the natural law—to prove, that is, at the bar of experience, that St. Francis does in fact enjoy a freer truth to essential human nature than Caligula, and that a society of Caligulas is more likely to end in catastrophe than a society of Franciscans.

Christian morality comprises both a moral code and a moral law. The Christian code is familiar to us; but we are apt to forget that it is valid or not valid according as Christian opinion is right or wrong about the moral law—that is to say, about the essential facts of human nature. Regulations about doing no murder and refraining from theft and adultery belong to the moral code and are based on certain opinions held by Christians in common about the value of human personality. Such "laws" as these are not statements of fact, but rules of behavior. Societies which do not share Christian opinion about human values are logically quite justified in repudiating the code based upon that opinion. If, however, Christian opinion turns out to be right about the facts of human nature, then the dissenting societies are exposing themselves to that judgment of catastrophe which awaits those who defy the natural law.

At the back of the Christian moral *code* we find a number of pronouncements about the moral *law*, which are not regulations at all, but which purport to be statements of fact about man and the universe, and upon which the whole moral code depends for its authority and its validity in practice. These statements do not rest on human consent; they are either true or false. If they are true, man runs counter to them at his own peril.[9] He may, of course, defy them, as he may defy the law of gravitation by jumping off the Eiffel Tower, but he cannot abolish them by edict. Nor yet can God abolish them, except by breaking up the structure of the universe, so that in this sense they are not arbitrary laws. We may of course argue that the making of this kind

[9] cf. the Virgilian concept of Destiny: "cosmic logic, which men are at liberty to flout if they choose, although, by so doing, they expose themselves to an inevitable penalty."—C. N. Cochrane: *Christianity and Classical Culture.*

of universe, or indeed of any kind of universe, is an arbitrary act; but, given the universe as it stands, the rules that govern it are not freaks of momentary caprice. There is a difference between saying: "If you hold your finger in the fire you will get burned" and saying, "if you whistle at your work I shall beat you, because the noise gets on my nerves." The God of the Christians is too often looked upon as an old gentleman of irritable nerves who beats people for whistling. This is the result of a confusion between arbitrary "law" and the "laws" which are statements of fact. Breach of the first is "punished" by edict; but breach of the second, by judgment.

"For He visits the sins of the fathers upon the children unto the third and fourth generation of them that hate Him, and shows mercy unto thousands of them that love Him and keep His commandments."

Here is a statement of fact, observed by the Jews and noted as such. From its phrasing it might appear an arbitrary expression of personal feeling. But today, we understand more about the mechanism of the universe, and are able to reinterpret the pronouncement by the "laws" of heredity and environment. Defy the commandments of the natural law, and the race will perish in a few generations; co-operate with them, and the race will flourish for ages to come. That is the fact; whether we like it or not, the universe is made that way. This commandment is interesting because it specifically puts forward the moral *law* as the basis of the moral *code: because* God has made the world like this and will not alter it, *therefore* you must not worship your own fantasies, but pay allegiance to the truth.

Scattered about the New Testament are other statements concerning the moral law, many of which bear a similar air of being arbitrary, harsh or paradoxical: "Whosoever will save his life shall lose it"; "to him that hath shall be given, but from him that hath not shall be taken away even that which he hath"; "it must needs be that offences come, but woe unto that man by whom the offence cometh"; "there is joy in heaven over one sinner that repenteth more than over ninety and nine just persons that need no repentance"; "it is easier for a camel to go through the eye of a needle than for a rich man to enter into the Kingdom of God"; "it is better for thee to enter halt into life than having two feet to be cast into hell"; "blasphemy against the Holy Ghost shall not be forgiven . . . neither in this world, neither in the world to come."

We may hear a saying such as these a thousand times, and find in it nothing but mystification and unreason; the thousand-and-first time, it falls into our recollection pat upon some vital experience, and we suddenly know it to be a statement of inexorable fact. The parable of the Unjust Steward presents an insoluble enigma when approached by way of a priori reasoning; it is only when we have personally wrestled with the oddly dishonest inefficiency of some of the children of light that we recognize its ironical truth to human nature. The cursing of the barren fig-tree looks like an outburst of irrational bad temper, "for it was not yet the time of figs"; till some desperate crisis confronts us with the challenge of that acted parable and we know that we must perform impossibilities or perish.

Of some laws such as these, psychology has already begun to expose the mechanism; on others, the only commentary yet available is that of life and history. It is essential to our understanding of all doctrine that we shall be able to distinguish between what is presented as personal opinion and what is presented as a judgment of fact. Twenty centuries ago, Aristotle, in his university lectures on poetry, offered certain observations on dramatic structure, which were subsequently codified as the "Rule of the Three Unities." These observations underwent the vicissitudes that attend all formal creeds. There was a period when they were held to be sacrosanct, not because they were a judgment of truth, but because they were the "say-so" of authority; and they were applied as tests automatically, regardless whether the actual plays in question were informed with the vital truth that was the reason behind the rule. Later, there was a reaction against them as against an arbitrary code, and critics of our own time have gone so far as to assert that Aristotle's unities are obsolete. But this is a folly worse than the other. Audiences who have never heard of Aristotle criticize plays every day for their failure to observe the unities. "The story," they say, "didn't seem to hang together; I didn't know whom to be interested in; it began as a drama and ended as a farce. . . . Too many scenes—the curtain was up one minute and down the next; I couldn't keep my attention fixed—all those intervals were so distracting. . . . The story is spread out over the whole Thirty Years' War; it would have been all right for a novel, but it wasn't concentrated enough for the theater; it just seemed to go on and on." What is the use of saying that twentieth-century playwrights should refuse to be bound by the dictum of an ancient Greek professor? They are bound, whether they

like it or not, by the fundamental realities of human
nature, which have not altered between classical Athens
and modern London. Aristotle never offered his "unities" as an *a priori* personal opinion about the abstract
ideal of a play: he offered them as observations of fact
about the kind of plays which were, in practice, successful. Judging by results, he put forward the observation
that the action of a play should be coherent and as concentrated as possible, otherwise—human nature being
what it is—the audience would become distracted and
bored. That is presented as a statement of fact—and
that it is a true statement of fact a melancholy succession
of theatrical failures bears witness to this day. It is open
to any playwright to reject Aristotle's opinion, but his
independence will not profit him if that opinion was
based on fact; it is open to any playwright to accept
Aristotle's opinion, but he ought to do so, not because
it is Aristotle's, but because the facts confirm it.

In a similar way, volumes of angry controversy have
been poured out about the Christian creeds, under the
impression that they represent, not statements of fact,
but arbitrary edicts. The conditions of salvation, for
instance, are discussed as though they were conditions
for membership in some fantastic club like the Red-
Headed League. They do not purport to be anything of
the kind. Rightly or wrongly, they purport to be necessary conditions based on the facts of human nature. We
are accustomed to find conditions attached to human
undertakings, some of which are arbitrary and some not.
A regulation that allowed a cook to make omelettes only
on condition of first putting on a top hat might conceiv-
ably be given the force of law, and penalties might be

inflicted for disobedience; but the condition would remain arbitrary and irrational. The law that omelettes can be made only on condition that there shall be a preliminary breaking of eggs is one with which we are sadly familiar. The efforts of idealists to make omelettes without observing that condition are foredoomed to failure by the nature of things. The Christian creeds are too frequently assumed to be in the top-hat category; this is an error; they belong to the category of egg-breaking. Even that most notorious of damnatory clauses which provokes sensitive ecclesiastics to defy the rubric and banish the Athanasian Creed from public recitation does not say that God will refuse to save unbelievers; it is at once less arbitrary and more alarming: "which except a man believe faithfully, he *cannot* be saved." It purports to be a statement of fact. The proper question to be asked about any creed is not, "Is it pleasant?" but, "is it true?" "Christianity has compelled the mind of man not because it is the most cheering view of man's existence but because it is truest to the facts." [10] It is unpleasant to be called sinners, and much nicer to think that we all have hearts of gold—but have we? It is agreeable to suppose that the more scientific knowledge we acquire the happier we shall be—but does it look like it? It is encouraging to feel that progress is making us automatically every day and in every way better, and better, and better—but does history support that view? "We hold these truths to be self-evident: that all men were created equal" [11]—but does the external evidence

[10] Lord David Cecil: "True and False Values": *The Fortnightly*, March 1940.
[11] Jefferson: Declaration of Independence.

support this *a priori* assertion? Or does experience rather suggest that man is "very far gone from original righteousness and is of his own nature inclined to evil"? [12]

A creed put forward by authority deserves respect in the measure that we respect the authority's claim to be a judge of truth. If the creed and the authority alike are conceived as being arbitrary, capricious and irrational, we shall continue in a state of terror and bewilderment, since we shall never know from one minute to the next what we are supposed to be doing, or why, or what we have to expect. But a creed that can be shown to have its basis in fact inclines us to trust the judgment of the authority; if in this case and in that it turns out to be correct, we may be disposed to think that it is, on the whole, probable that it is correct about everything. The necessary condition for assessing the value of creeds is that we should fully understand that they claim to be, not idealistic fancies, not arbitrary codes, not abstractions irrelevant to human life and thought, but statements of fact about the universe as we know it. Any witness—however small—to the rationality of a creed assists us to an intelligent apprehension of what it is intended to mean, and enables us to decide whether it is, or is not, as it sets out to be, a witness of universal truth.

[12] Church of England: *Articles of Religion*, IX.

II

THE IMAGE OF GOD

Those things which are said of God and other things are predicated neither univocally nor equivocally, but analogically. . . . *Accordingly, since we arrive at the knowledge of God from other things, the reality of the names predicated of God and other things is first in God according to His mode, but the meaning of the name is in Him afterwards. Wherefore He is said to be named from His effects.*

—ST. THOMAS AQUINAS: *Summa contra Gentiles*

We have torn away the mental fancies to get at the reality beneath, only to find that the reality of that which is beneath is bound up with its potentiality of awakening these fancies. It is because the mind, the weaver of illusion, is also the only guarantor of reality that reality is always to be sought at the base of illusion.

—SIR ARTHUR EDDINGTON: *Nature of the Physical World*

THE IMAGE OF GOD

IN the beginning God created. He made this and He made that and He saw that it was good. And He created man in His own image; in the image of God created He him; male and female created He them.

Thus far the author of *Genesis*. The expression "in His own image" has occasioned a good deal of controversy. Only the most simple-minded people of any age or nation have supposed the image to be a physical one. The innumerable pictures which display the Creator as a hirsute old gentleman in flowing robes seated on a bank of cloud are recognized to be purely symbolic. The "image," whatever the author may have meant by it, is something shared by male and female alike; the aggressive masculinity of the pictorial Jehovah represents power, rationality or what you will: it has no relation to the text I have quoted. Christian doctrine and tradition, indeed, by language and picture, sets its face against all sexual symbolism for the divine fertility. Its Trinity is wholly masculine, as all language relating to Man as a species is masculine.[1]

The Jews, keenly alive to the perils of pictorial metaphor, forbade the representation of the Person of God in graven images. Nevertheless, human nature and the nature of human language defeated them. No legislation could prevent the making of verbal pictures: God walks

---

[1] cf. St. Augustine: *On the Trinity;* Bk. XII, Chap. V.

in the garden, He stretches out His arm, His voice shakes the cedars, His eyelids try the children of men. To forbid the making of pictures about God would be to forbid thinking about God at all, for man is so made that he has no way to think except in pictures. But continually, throughout the history of the Jewish-Christian Church, the voice of warning has been raised against the power of the picture-makers: "God is a spirit," [2] "without body, parts or passions;" [3] He is pure being, "I AM THAT I AM." [4]

Man, very obviously, is not a being of this kind; his body, parts and passions are only too conspicuous in his make-up. How then can he be said to resemble God? Is it his immortal soul, his rationality, his self-consciousness, his free will, or what, that gives him a claim to this rather startling distinction? A case may be argued for all these elements in the complex nature of man. But had the author of *Genesis* anything particular in his mind when he wrote? It is observable that in the passage leading up to the statement about man, he has given no detailed information about God. Looking at man, he sees in him something essentially divine, but when we turn back to see what he says about the original upon which the "image" of God was modeled, we find only the single assertion, "God created." The characteristic common to God and man is apparently that: the desire and the ability to make things.

This, we may say, is a metaphor like other statements about God. So it is, but it is none the worse for that. All language about God must, as St. Thomas Aquinas

[2] St. John iv. 24.
[3] *Articles of Religion*, I.
[4] Exodus iv. 14.

pointed out, necessarily be analogical. We need not be surprised at this, still less suppose that because it is analogical it is therefore valueless or without any relation to the truth. The fact is, that all language about everything is analogical; we think in a series of metaphors. We can explain nothing in terms of itself, but only in terms of other things. Even mathematics can express itself in terms of itself only so long as it deals with an ideal system of pure numbers; the moment it begins to deal with numbers of *things* it is forced back into the language of analogy. In particular, when we speak about something of which we have no direct experience, we must think by analogy or refrain from thought. It may be perilous, as it must be inadequate, to interpret God by analogy with ourselves, but we are compelled to do so; we have no other means of interpreting anything. Skeptics frequently complain that man has made God in his own image; they should in reason go further (as many of them do) and acknowledge that man has made all existence in his own image. If the tendency to anthropomorphism is a good reason for refusing to think about God, it is an equally good reason for refusing to think about light, or oysters, or battleships. It may quite well be perilous, as it must be inadequate, to interpret the mind of our pet dog by analogy with ourselves; we can by no means enter directly into the nature of a dog; behind the appealing eyes and the wagging tail lies a mystery as inscrutable as the mystery of the Trinity. But that does not prevent us from ascribing to the dog feelings and ideas based on analogy with our own experience; and our behavior to the dog, controlled by this kind of experimental guesswork, produces practical results which are reasonably satisfactory. Similarly the physicist, struggling to interpret the alien structure of the atom, finds himself obliged to consider it sometimes as a "wave" and sometimes as a "particle." He knows very well that both these terms are analogical—they are metaphors, "picture-thinking," and, as pictures, they are incompatible and mutually contradictory. But he need not on that account refrain from using them for what they are worth. If he were to wait till he could have immediate experience of the atom, he would have to wait until he was set free from the framework of the universe.[5] In the meantime, so long as he remembers that language and observation are human functions, partaking at every point of the limitations of humanity, he can get along quite well with them and carry out fruitful researches. To complain that man measures God by his own experience is a waste of time; man measures everything by his own experience; he has no other yardstick.

We have, then, various analogies by which we seek to interpret to ourselves the nature of God as it is known to us by experience. Sometimes we speak of Him as a king, and use metaphors drawn from that analogy. We talk, for instance, of His kingdom, laws, dominion, service and soldiers. Still more frequently, we speak of Him as a father, and think it quite legitimate to argue from the analogy of human fatherhood to the "father-

[5] Research forces us to think far beyond the limits of the imagination. Formulae afford the medium of expressing the new discoveries, but the imagination is incapable of conveying the particular reality to our mind. The confident "it is" is reduced to a hesitating "it appears to be." A process appears to be the action of waves or of particles depending on the angle from which it is viewed. Dispense with formulae to express a scientific generalization and only analogy remains.—Huizinga: *In the Shadow of To-morrow.*

hood" of God. This particular "picture-thought" is one of which Christ was very fond, and it has stamped itself indelibly on the language of Christian worship and doctrine: "God the Father Almighty," "like as a father pitieth his own children," "your Father in Heaven careth for you," "the children of God," "the Son of God," "as many as are led by the spirit of God are sons of God," "I will arise and go to my father," "Our Father which art in Heaven." In books and sermons we express the relation between God and mankind in terms of human parenthood; we say that, just as a father is kind, careful, unselfish and forgiving in his dealings with his children, so is God in his dealings with men; that there is a true likeness of nature between God and man as between a father and his sons; and that because we are sons of one Father, we should look on all men as our brothers.

When we use these expressions, we know perfectly well that they are metaphors and analogies; what is more, we know perfectly well where the metaphor begins and ends. We do not suppose for one moment that God procreates children in the same manner as a human father and we are quite well aware that preachers who use the "father" metaphor intend and expect no such perverse interpretation of their language. Nor (unless we are very stupid indeed) do we go on to deduce from the analogy that we are to imagine God as being a cruel, careless or injudicious father such as we may see from time to time in daily life; still less, that *all* the activities of a human father may be attributed to God, such as earning money for the support of the family or demanding the first use of the bathroom in the morning. Our own common sense assures us that the metaphor is intended to be drawn from the best kind of father acting within a certain limited sphere of behavior, and is to be applied only to a well-defined number of the divine attributes.

I have put down these very elementary notes on the limitations of metaphor, because this book is an examination of metaphors about God, and because it is well to remind ourselves before we begin of the way in which metaphorical language—that is to say, all language—is properly used. It is an expression of experience and of the relation of one experience to the other. Further, its meaning is realized only in experience. We frequently say, "Until I had that experience, I never knew what the word fear (or love, or anger, or whatever it is) *meant*." The language, which had been merely pictorial, is transmuted into experience and we then have immediate knowledge of the reality behind the picture.

The words of creeds come before our eyes and ears as pictures; we do not apprehend them as statements of experience; it is only when our own experience is brought into relation with the experience of the men who framed the creeds that we are able to say: "I recognize that for a statement of experience; I know now what the words mean."

The analogical statements of experience which I want to examine are those used by the Christian creeds about God the Creator.

And first of all, is the phrase "God the Creator" metaphorical in the same sense that "God the Father" is clearly metaphorical? At first sight, it does not appear to be so. We know what a human father is, but what is a human creator? We are very well aware that man cannot create in the absolute sense in which we understand the word when we apply it to God. We say that "He made the world out of nothing," but we cannot ourselves make anything out of nothing. We can only rearrange the unalterable and indestructible units of matter in the universe and build them up into new forms. We might reasonably say that in the "father" metaphor we are arguing from the known to the unknown; whereas, in the "creator" metaphor, we are arguing from the unknown to the unknowable.

But to say this is to overlook the metaphorical nature of all language. We use the word "create" to convey an extension and amplification of something that we do know, and we limit the application of the metaphor precisely as we limit the application of the metaphor of fatherhood. We know a father and picture to ourselves an ideal Father; similarly, we know a human "maker" and picture to ourselves an ideal "Maker." If the word "Maker" does not mean something related to our human experience of making, then it has no meaning at all. We extend it to the concept of a Maker who can make something out of nothing; we limit it to exclude the concept of employing material tools. It is analogical language simply because it is human language, and it is related to human experience for the same reason.

This particular metaphor has been much less studied than the metaphor of "the Father." This is partly because the image of divine Fatherhood has been particularly consecrated by Christ's use of it; partly because most of us have a very narrow experience of the act of creation. It is true that everybody is a "maker" in the simplest meaning of the term. We spend our lives putting matter together in new patterns and so "creating" forms which were not there before. This is so intimate and universal a function of nature that we scarcely ever think about it. In a sense, even this kind of creation is "creation out of nothing." Though we cannot create matter, we continually, by rearrangement, create new and unique entities. A million buttons, stamped out by machine, though they may be exactly alike, are not the *same* button; with each separate act of making, an entity has appeared in the world that was not there before. Nevertheless, we perceive that this is only a very poor and restricted kind of creation. We acknowledge a richer experience in the making of an individual and original work. By a metaphor vulgar but corresponding to a genuine experience, we speak of a model hat or gown as a "creation": it is unique, not merely by its entity but by its individuality. Again, by another natural metaphor, we may call a perfectly prepared beefsteak pudding, "a work of art"; and in these words we acknowledge an analogy with what we instinctively feel to be a still more satisfying kind of "creation."

It is the artist who, more than other men, is able to create something out of nothing. A whole artistic work is immeasurably more than the sum of its parts.

But here is the will of God, a flash of the will that can,
    Existent behind all laws, that made them, and lo, they are!
And I know not if, save in this, such gift be allowed to man,
    That out of three sounds he frame, not a fourth sound,
        but a star.

Consider it well: each tone of our scale in itself is nought,
  It is everywhere in the world—loud, soft, and all is said:
Give it to me to use! I mix it with two in my thought:
  And there! Ye have heard and seen: consider and bow the
    head! [6]

"I mix it with two *in my thought*"; this is the statement of the fact of universal experience that the work of art has real existence apart from its translation into material form. Without the thought, though the material parts already exist, the form does not and cannot. The "creation" is not a product of the matter, and is not simply a rearrangement of the matter. The amount of matter in the universe is limited, and its possible rearrangements, though the sum of them would amount to astronomical figures, is also limited. But no such limitation of numbers applies to the creation of works of art. The poet is not obliged, as it were, to destroy the material of a Hamlet in order to create a Falstaff, as a carpenter must destroy a tree-form to create a table-form. The components of the material world are fixed; those of the world of imagination increase by a continuous and irreversible process, without any destruction or rearrangement of what went before. This represents the nearest approach we experience to "creation out of nothing," and we conceive of the act of absolute creation as being an act analogous to that of the creative artist. Thus Berdyaev is able to say: "God created the world by imagination."

This experience of the creative imagination in the common man or woman and in the artist is the only thing we have to go upon in entertaining and formulat-

[6] Robert Browning: *Abt Vogler.*

ing the concept of creation. Outside our own experience of procreation and creation we can form no notion of how anything comes into being. The expressions "God the Father" and "God the Creator" are thus seen to belong to the same category—that is, of analogies based on human experience, and limited or extended by a similar mental process in either case.

If all this is true, then it is to the creative artists that we should naturally turn for an exposition of what is *meant* by those credal formulae which deal with the nature of the Creative Mind. Actually, we seldom seem to consult them in the matter. Poets have, indeed, often communicated in their own mode of expression truths identical with the theologians' truths; but just because of the difference in the modes of expression, we often fail to see the identity of the statements. The artist does not recognize that the phrases of the creeds purport to be observations of fact about the creative mind *as such*, including his own; while the theologian, limiting the application of the phrases to the divine Maker, neglects to inquire of the artist what light he can throw upon them from his own immediate apprehension of truth. The confusion is as though two men were to argue fiercely whether there was a river in a certain district or whether, on the contrary, there was a measurable volume of H_2O moving in a particular direction with an ascertainable velocity; neither having any suspicion that they were describing the same phenomenon.

Our minds are not infinite; and as the volume of the world's knowledge increases, we tend more and more to confine ourselves, each to his special sphere of interest and to the specialized metaphor belonging to it.

The analytic bias of the last three centuries has immensely encouraged this tendency, and it is now very difficult for the artist to speak the language of the theologian or the scientist the language of either. But the attempt must be made; and there are signs everywhere that the human mind is once more beginning to move towards a synthesis of experience.

III

IDEA, ENERGY, POWER

. . . because the image of the Trinity was made in man, that in this way man should be the image of the one true God.
— ST. AUGUSTINE: *On the Trinity*

To God, as Godhead, appertain neither will, nor knowledge, nor manifestation, nor anything that we can name, or say, or conceive. But to God, as God, it belongeth to express Himself, and to know and love Himself, and to reveal Himself to Himself; and all this without any creature. . . . And without the creature, this would lie in His own Self as a Substance or well-spring, but would not be manifested or wrought out into deeds. Now God will have it to be exercised and clothed in a form . . . and this cannot come to pass . . . without the creature. — *Theologia Germanica*

In thought, the sense of the setting and one's knowledge of the characters are all present simultaneously. In writing, something of these elements has to be conveyed in sequence.
— J. D. BERESFORD: *Writing Aloud*

IDEA, ENERGY, POWER

I SUPPOSE that of all Christian dogmas, the doctrine of the Trinity enjoys the greatest reputation for obscurity and remoteness from common experience. Whether the theologian extols it as the splendor of the light invisible or the skeptic derides it as a horror of great darkness, there is a general conspiracy to assume that its effect upon those who contemplate it is blindness, either by absence or excess of light. There is some truth in the assumption, but there is also a great deal of exaggeration. God is mysterious, and so (for that matter) is the universe and one's fellow-man and one's self and the snail on the garden-path; but none of these is so mysterious as to correspond to nothing within human knowledge. There are, of course, some minds that cultivate mystery for mystery's sake: with these, St. Augustine of Hippo, who was no obscurantist, deals firmly:

Holy Scripture, which suits itself to babes, has not avoided words drawn from any class of things really existing, through which, as by nourishment, our understanding might rise gradually to things divine and transcendent. . . . But it has drawn no words whatever, whereby to frame either figures of speech or enigmatic sayings, from things which do not exist at all. And hence it is that those who [in disputing about God strive to transcend the whole creation] are more mischievously and emptily vain than their fellows;

in that they surmise concerning God, what can neither be found in Himself nor in any creature.[1]

He proceeds, in his great treatise, to expound the doctrine analogically, using again and again the appeal to experience. He says in effect: "a Trinitarian structure of being is not a thing incomprehensible or unfamiliar to you; you know of many such within the created universe. There is a trinity of sight, for example: the form seen, the act of vision, and the mental attention which correlates the two. These three, though separable in theory, are inseparably present whenever you use your sight. Again, every thought is an inseparable trinity of memory, understanding, and will.[2] This is a fact of which you are quite aware; it is not the concept of a trinity-in-unity that in itself presents any insuperable difficulty to the human imagination."

We may perhaps go so far as to assert that the Trinitarian structure of activity is mysterious to us just because it is universal—rather as the four-dimensional structure of space-time is mysterious because we cannot get outside it to look at it. The mathematician can, however, to some extent perform the intellectual feat of observing space-time from without, and we may similarly call upon the creative artist to extricate himself from his own activity far enough to examine and describe its threefold structure.

For the purpose of this examination I shall use the

[1] *On the Trinity:* Bk. I, Chap. I.
[2] cf. Eddington, *Philosophy of Physical Science:* "Still less is a single sensation strictly separable from the environment of emotion, memory and intellectual activity in which it occurs; nor is it strictly separable from the volition which directs attention to it and the thought which embodies sapient knowledge of it."

mind of the creative writer, both because I am more familiar with its workings than with those of other creative artists, and because I shall thus save the confusion of a great many clauses beginning with "and" and "or." But, *mutatis mutandis*, what is true of the writer is true also of the painter, the musician and all workers of creative imagination in whatever form. "The writer" is of course understood to be the ideal writer, considered when engaged in an act of artistic creation, just as, in considering the "father" we always intend the ideal parent, considered while exercising the functions of parenthood and in no other activity. It is not to be imagined that any human writer ever works with ideal perfection; in the tenth chapter of this book I shall try to point out what happens when the writer's trinity fails too conspicuously to conform to the law of its own nature—for here, as always, there is a judgment for behavior that runs counter to the law.

Since this chapter—and indeed this whole book—is an expansion of the concluding speech of St. Michael in my play *The Zeal of Thy House*, it will perhaps be convenient to quote that speech here:

For every work [*or act*] of creation is threefold, an earthly trinity to match the heavenly.

First, [*not in time, but merely in order of enumeration*] there is the Creative Idea, passionless, timeless, beholding the whole work complete at once, the end in the beginning: and this is the image of the Father.

Second, there is the Creative Energy [*or Activity*] begotten of that idea, working in time from the beginning to the end, with sweat and passion, being incarnate in the bonds of matter: and this is the image of the Word.

Third, there is the Creative Power, the meaning of the

work and its response in the lively soul: and this is the image of the indwelling Spirit.

And these three are one, each equally in itself the whole work, whereof none can exist without other: and this is the image of the Trinity.

Of these clauses, the one which gives the most trouble to the hearer is that dealing with the Creative Idea. (The word is here used, not in the philosopher's sense, in which the "Idea" tends to be equated with the "Word," but quite simply in the sense intended by the writer when he says: "I have an idea for a book." [3]) The ordinary man is apt to say: "I thought you began by collecting material and working out the plot." The confusion here is not merely over the words "first" and "begin." In fact the "Idea"—or rather the writer's realization of his own idea—does precede any mental or physical work upon the materials or on the course of the story within a time-series. But apart from this, the very formulation of the Idea in the writer's mind is not the Idea itself, but its self-awareness in the Energy. Everything that is conscious, everything that has to do with form and time, and everything that has to do with process, belongs to the working of the Energy or Activity or "Word." The Idea, that is, cannot be said to precede the Energy in time, because (so far as that act of creation is concerned) it is the Energy that creates the time-process. This is the analogy of the theological expressions that "the Word was in the beginning with God" and was "eter-

[3] Similarly, of course, "Energy" is not to be understood in the physicist's technical sense (e.g., Mass × Acceleration × Distance), or "Power" in the engineer's sense (e.g., applied force); both these words are used in the sense intended by the poet and the common man.

nally begotten of the Father." If, that is, the act has a beginning in time at all, it is because of the presence of the Energy or Activity. The writer cannot even be conscious of his Idea except by the working of the Energy which formulates it to himself.

That being so, how can we know that the Idea itself has any real existence apart from the Energy? Very strangely; by the fact that the Energy itself is conscious of referring all its acts to an existing and complete whole. In theological terms, the Son does the will of the Father. Quite simply, every choice of an episode, or a phrase. or a word is made to conform to a pattern of the entire book, which is revealed by that choice as already existing. This truth, which is difficult to convey in explanation, is quite clear and obvious in experience. It manifests itself plainly enough when the writer says or thinks: "That is, or is not, the right phrase"—meaning that it is a phrase which does or does not correspond to the reality of the Idea.

Further, although the book—that is, the activity of writing the book—is a process in space and time, it is known to the writer as *also* a complete and timeless whole, "the end in the beginning," and this knowledge of it is with him always, while writing it and after it is finished, just as it was at the beginning. It is not changed or affected by the toils and troubles of composition, nor is the writer aware of his book as merely a succession of words and situations. The Idea of the book is a thing-in-itself quite apart from its awareness or its manifestation in Energy, though it still remains true that it cannot be known as a thing-in-itself except as the Energy reveals it. The Idea is thus timeless and without parts or passions, though it is never seen, either by writer or reader, except in terms of time, parts and passion.

The Energy itself is an easier concept to grasp, because it is the thing of which the writer is conscious and which the reader can see when it is manifest in material form. It is dynamic—the sum and process of all the activity which brings the book into temporal and spatial existence. "All things are made by it, and without it nothing is made that has been made." To it belongs everything that can be included under the word "passion"—feeling, thought, toil, trouble, difficulty, choice, triumph—all the accidents which attend a manifestation in time. It is the Energy that is the creator in the sense in which the common man understands the word, because it brings about an expression in temporal form of the eternal and immutable Idea. It is, for the writer, what he means by "the writing of the book," and it includes, though it is not confined to, the manifestation of the book in material form. We shall have more to say about it in the following chapters: for the moment, the thing I am anxious to establish is that it is something distinct from the Idea itself, though it is the only thing that can make the Idea known to itself or to others, and yet is (in the ideal creative act which we are considering) essentially identical with the Idea—"consubstantial with the Father."

The Creative Power is the third "Person" of the writer's trinity. It is not the same thing as the Energy (which for greater clearness I ought perhaps to have called "the Activity"), though it proceeds from the Idea and the Energy together. It is the thing which flows back to the writer from his own activity and makes him,

as it were, the reader of his own book. It is also, of
course, the means by which the Activity is communicated to other readers and which produces a corresponding response in them. In fact, from the reader's point of
view, it *is* the book. By it, they perceive the book, both
as a process in time and as an eternal whole, and react
to it dynamically. It is at this point we begin to understand what St. Hilary means in saying of the Trinity:
"Eternity is in the Father, form in the Image and use in
the Gift."

Lastly: "these three are one, each equally in itself
the whole work, whereof none can exist without other."
If you were to ask a writer which is "the real book"—
his Idea of it, his Activity in writing it, or its return
to himself in Power, he would be at a loss to tell you,
because these things are essentially inseparable. Each of
them is the complete book separately; yet in the complete book all of them exist together. He can, by an act
of the intellect, "distinguish the persons" but he cannot
by any means "divide the substance." How could he?
He cannot know the Idea, except by the Power interpreting his own Activity to him; he knows the Activity
only as it reveals the Idea in Power; he knows the Power
only as the revelation of the Idea in the Activity. All
he can say is that these three are equally and eternally
present in his own act of creation, and at every moment
of it, whether or not the act ever becomes manifest in
the form of a written and printed book. These things
are not confined to the material manifestation: they exist
in—they *are*—the creative mind itself.

I ought perhaps to emphasize this point a little. The
whole complex relation that I have been trying to de-

scribe may remain entirely within the sphere of the imagination, and is there complete. The Trinity abides and works and is responsive to itself "in Heaven." A writer may be heard to say: "My book is finished—I have only to write it"; or even, "My book is written—I have only to put it on paper." The creative act, that is, does not depend for its fulfillment upon its manifestation in a material creation. The glib assertion that "God needs His creation as much as His creation needs Him" is not a true analogy from the mind of the human creator. Nevertheless, it is true that the urgent desire of the creative mind is towards expression in material form. The writer, in writing his book on paper, is expressing the freedom of his own nature in accordance with the law of his being; and we argue from this that material creation expresses the nature of the Divine Imagination. We may perhaps say that creation in some form or another is necessary to the nature of God; what we cannot say is that this or any particular form of creation is necessary to Him. It is in His mind, complete, whether He writes it down or not. To say that God depends on His creation as a poet depends on his written poem is an abuse of metaphor: the poet does nothing of the sort. To write the poem (or, of course, to give it material form in speech or song), is an act of love towards the poet's own imaginative act and towards his fellow-beings. It is a social act; but the poet is, first and foremost, his own society, and would be none the less a poet if the means of material expression were refused by him or denied him.

I have used in this chapter, and shall use again, expressions which to persons brought up in "scientific" habits of thought may seem to be out-moded. Scientists are growing more and more chary of using any forms of speech at all. Words like "idea," "matter," "existence," and their derivatives have become suspect. "Old truths have to be abandoned, general terms of everyday use which we thought to be the keys to understanding will now no longer fit the lock. Evolution, yes, but be very careful with it, for the concept is slightly rusty. Elements . . . their immutability no longer exists. Causation . . . on the whole there is little one can do with the concept; it breaks at the slightest usage. Natural laws . . . certainly, but better not talk too much of absolute validity. Objectivity . . . it is still our duty as well as our ideal, but its perfect realization is not possible, at least not for the social sciences and the humanities." [4]

This difficulty which confronts the scientists and has compelled their flight into formulae is the result of a failure to understand or accept the analogical nature of language. Men of science spend much time and effort in the attempt to disentangle words from their metaphorical and traditional associations; the attempt is bound to prove vain since it runs counter to the law of humanity.[5] The confusion and difficulty are increased by the modern world's preoccupation with the concept of progress. This concept—now rapidly becoming as precarious as those others quoted by Huizinga—imposes upon the human mind two (in the hypnotic sense) "suggestions." The first is that any invention or creative act will necessarily tend to supersede an act of earlier date. This may be true of mechanical inventions and scientific formulae:

[4] Huizinga: *In the Shadow of To-morrow.*
[5] See Note "A" at end of chapter.

we may say, for example, that the power-loom has superseded the hand-loom, or that Einsteinian physics has
superseded Newtonian physics, and mean something by
saying so. But there is no sense whatever in which we
can say that *Hamlet* has "superseded" the *Agamemnon*,
or that

> you who were with me in the ships at Mylae

has superseded

> en la sua voluntade è nostra pace

or

> tendebantque manus ripae ulterioris amore.

The later in date leaves the earlier achievement uncon-
quered and unchanged; that which was at the summit
remains at the summit until the end of time.

The second suggestion is that, once an invention has
been brought into being and made public by a creative
act, the whole level of human understanding is raised to
the level of that inventiveness. This is not true, even
within its own sphere of application. The fact that every
schoolboy can now use logarithms does not lift him to
the intellectual level of the brain that first imagined the
method of logarithmic calculation. But the absurdity of
the suggestion becomes glaringly obvious when we consider the arts. If a ruthless education in Shakespeare's
language could produce a nation of Shakespeares, every
Englishman would at this moment be a dramatic genius.
Actually, all that such an education can possibly do is
to improve a little the general apparatus of linguistic
machinery and so make the way smooth for the appearance of the still rare, still incalculable genius. Genius is,

in fact, not subject to the "law" of progress, and it is beginning to be extremely doubtful whether progress is a "law" at all.

For these reasons, we need not allow ourselves to be abashed by any suggestion that the old metaphors are out of date and ought to be superseded. We have only to remember that they are, and always were, metaphors, and that they are still "living" metaphors so long as we use them to interpret direct experience. Metaphors become dead only when the metaphor is substituted for the experience, and the argument carried on in a sphere of abstraction without being at every point related to life.

In the metaphors used by the Christian creeds about the mind of the maker, the creative artist can recognize a true relation to his own experience; and it is his business to record the fact of that recognition in any further metaphor that the reader may understand and apply.

NOTE "A"—*Analogical Nature of Language*

"Suppose that I suddenly say 'Ouch.' That will convey to you exactly what was meant to be conveyed by the former statement 'I feel pain.' It has the great advantage that it does not hint at any psychological theory of what has happened; it does not drag in knowledge not wholly derived from direct awareness, as any attempt at precise description would do. Normally, it is an involuntary remark; but it is a pity not to use deliberately an expression which conveys exactly what we mean to convey and no more. A typical element of knowledge acquired by direct awareness is that which we convey to another person by the ejaculation 'Ouch.' "   —Eddington: *Philosophy of Physical Science*

It is noteworthy that certain schools of poetry in the present "scientific" age (e.g., expressionists, dadaists, surrealists) appear to suffer precisely this same embarrassment in dealing with the analogical nature of language, and use their best endeavors to convey all awareness of experience in terms of "ouch." This attempt to escape from the tradition and nature of its own instrument is of very dubious value; cf. also Huizinga: *In the Shadow of To-morrow*, Chap. 18: "Art and Literature"

IV

THE ENERGY REVEALED IN CREATION

We behold, then, by the sight of the mind, in that eternal truth from which all things temporal are made, the form according to which we are, and according to which we do anything by true and right reason, either in ourselves, or in things corporeal; and we have the true knowledge of things, thence conceived, as it were as a word within us, and by speaking we beget it from within; nor by being born does it depart from us. And when we speak to others, we apply to the word, remaining within us, the ministry of the voice or of some bodily sign, that by some kind of sensible remembrance some similar thing may be wrought also in the mind of him that hears,—similar, I say, to that which does not depart from the mind of him that speaks. . . . And this word is conceived by love, either of the creature or of the Creator, that is, either of changeable nature or of unchangeable truth. —ST. AUGUSTINE: *On the Trinity*

THE ENERGY REVEALED IN CREATION

AS soon as the mind of the maker has been made manifest in a work, a way of communication is established between other minds and his. That is to say, it is possible for a reader, by reading a book, to discover something about the mind of the writer. And it is interesting to see how, in a minor way, the same difficulties and misunderstandings which are encountered in establishing communication with God crop up in the apparently much simpler matter of communication between writer and reader. The chief riddle that perplexes the common man is that paradox which theologians formulate in the statement that "God is both immanent and transcendent." Is it true, as the Pantheists assert, that the creator is simply the sum of all his works, or, on the other hand, is he something entirely detached from the work he has made and so unknowable in himself that the work provides us with no clue to his personality?

If we put the question like this and apply it analogically to a writer, most people will readily agree that both hypotheses are obviously false. We cannot put our hand on the fat volume containing Shakespeare's Plays and say that this is all there ever was, is, or will be of William Shakespeare. Quite apart from the private activities of Shakespeare, we know very well that his mind must have contained the stuff of many more potential plays, which presumably remained within the heaven of his imagination and were never made manifest in a written work. The mind of Shakespeare, we shall readily admit, transcends his work—transcends, that is, his whole work, not merely any one play or any one character in that play. The suggestion that it does not, seems (when we look at it that way) ridiculous.

And yet, in practice, we are continually tempted to confine the mind of the writer to its expression within his creation, particularly if it suits our purpose to do so. We try to identify him with this or that part of his works, as though it contained his whole mind. We do this, most notoriously and most absurdly, with playwrights. Hamlet, we say, "is" Shakespeare himself. Or we remark: As Shakespeare says,

"The evil that men do lives after them,
The good is oft interred with their bones"—

quite regardless of the fact that this remark was not made by Shakespeare personally, but put by him into the mouth of a man making a political speech. The accusation of unwarrantable optimism, deaf and blind to the world's suffering, is brought against Browning largely on the strength of

"God's in His Heaven,
All's right with the world"—

the song sung by Pippa in a dramatic poem which deals fairly drastically with adultery, treachery, conspiracy to murder and other such unamiable aspects of human society.

We are rather eclectic about these identifications. We seldom bolster up our worst designs with the observation: "As Milton says, 'Evil, be thou my good,' " or conclude that because Shakespeare created Iago, therefore he "was" Iago. But we do incline to suppose that a writer can be somehow cabined, cribbed, confined inside one of his "favorite" characters or one of his more impassioned utterances.

The reader is, of course, right thus far: that a writer cannot create a character or express a thought or emotion which is not within his own mind. (It will be remembered that we are dealing with an ideal writer; it is always possible for a man to put on paper sentiments and characteristics that are not sincere expressions of himself but merely derivative. Even then, though the manufactured stereotype betrays itself by its falsity, it remains a true expression of an intrinsic spiritual falsity within the writer.) Shakespeare is Iago as well as Othello; he can create the one as well as the other, because each is to some extent an expression of himself.

Actually (for those who are interested in the machinery of verbal creation) what happens in the writer's mind is something like this. When making a character he in a manner separates and incarnates a part of his own living mind. He recognizes in himself a powerful emotion—let us say, jealousy. His activity then takes this form: Supposing this emotion were to become so strong as to dominate my whole personality, how should I feel and how should I behave? In imagination he becomes the jealous person and thinks and feels within that frame of experience, so that the jealousy of Othello is the true creative expression of the jealousy of Shakespeare. He follows out, in fact, the detective system employed by Chesterton's "Father Brown":

"I mean that I really did see myself, and my real self, committing the murders. . . . I mean that I thought and thought about how a man might come to be like that, until I realised that I really *was* like that, in everything except actual final consent to the action." [1]

In this sense, therefore, Shakespeare "is" Othello; but we must allow that he "is," in the same sense, Coriolanus and Iago, Lear and Cordelia and every other character in his plays, from Hamlet down to Caliban. Or perhaps it would be more in accordance with reality to say that all these characters "are" Shakespeare—externalizations of some part of the writer's self and self-experience.

It is also true, as the reader's critical faculty recognizes, that the writer has "favorite" characters, which seem to embody more of or more important parts of his personality than the rest. These are, as it were, the saints and prophets of his art, who speak by inspiration. The creative act is here one of extreme delicacy, and in studying it we gain a kind of illumination upon the variety and inconclusiveness of the world about us. For if a character becomes *merely* a mouthpiece of the author, he ceases to be a character, and is no longer a living creation. Still more, if *all* the characters speak with their author's voice, the whole work loses its reality, and with it, its power. We sometimes complain, for example, that "all Oscar Wilde's characters talk like Oscar Wilde," and in saying so we know that we are uttering a condemnation of the work and accusing it of a kind of shallowness or brittleness which damages its claim to be a real act of creative power. This is not wholly because of a certain shallowness and brittleness in the mind of

[1] G. K. Chesterton: *The Secret of Father Brown.*

Wilde—we should feel exactly the same about a work in which all the characters spoke like the Prophet Isaiah. The vital power of an imaginative work demands a diversity within its unity; and the stronger the diversity, the more massive the unity. Incidentally, this is the weakness of most "edifying" or "propaganda" literature. There is no diversity. The Energy is active only in one part of the whole, and in consequence the wholeness is destroyed and the Power diminished. You cannot, in fact, give God His due without giving the devil his due also. This strange paradox is bound up with the problem of free will among the characters, to which we shall return later. At the moment we will merely note the fact that a creative work in which all the characters automatically reproduce a single aspect of the writer's mind is a work lacking in creative power. We may also consider the bearing of this fact on the concept of a Utopia, and on the question why, if there had to be a universe, it could not be one which automatically fulfilled the will of its Maker.

The writer, then, if—under the conditions we know— he is to perform an act of power in creation, must allow his Energy to enter with an equal fullness into all his creatures, whatever portions of his personality they emphasize and embody. Not only must his sensitiveness find energetic expression in Hamlet; his insensitiveness must also enter energetically into Rosencrantz and Guildenstern. We all have moments when we desire to take refuge in convention and stand well with every man, and those moments, if the writer will actively embody them in created form, will issue in a true creation—brief and trifling, perhaps, but instinct with power. This is the

writer's necessity, no matter what he is writing, and
whether his diversity is expressed in the creation of character or merely in the creation of an impersonal argument.

The writer himself becomes intensely conscious of
this necessity when, after some years spent in other kinds
of writing, he attempts to write for the stage. In writing
a novel, for example, it is only too easy for him to neglect this process of self-expression where minor characters are concerned. Let us say that the situation calls for
a dialogue among four or five persons. It is probable that
the central character will, so far as he goes, represent a
true act of creation: the author will have "entered into
him," and his words will be a lively expression of his
creator's emotion and experience. But some or all of the
other personages may be mere dummies, whose only
function is to return the verbal ball to the chief speaker's
hand. In that case, the creative act is a failure, so far as
they are concerned; in them, the Energy is not incarnate; they do not, as we say, "come to life," and as a result of the failure of the Energy to create, no Power
flows out upon or from them. The reader and indeed the
writer himself, may not notice this very much in reading
a novel; but in writing for the stage the failure becomes
very apparent, because the actors who have to play the
minor parts become instantly aware that the "characters" are not there for them to play. The Energy has not
entered into the lines and in consequence, no Power
communicates itself to the interpreters. If such a devital-
ized character is represented in the theater, any Power
that flows from it to the audience can then issue only
from the Energy of the actor himself, "creating" the

part as well as he may, in accordance with such Idea as he may have been able to find within the resources of his own mind.

The good playwright with dramatic sense—one, that is, who understands the necessity of informing all his characters with his proper vitality—goes through a very curious experience when writing dialogue. He feels within himself a continual shifting of his Energy from the one character to the other as he writes. He is usually (I think) aware of the stage itself in his imagination; by an act of mental vision he disposes his characters upon it, and his center of consciousness shifts as he goes, so that in writing down John's lines he seems to view the stage from John's point of view, while in writing Mary's reply he views it from Mary's point of view. At the same time, he knows quite well that his responsive Power is sitting, so to speak, in the audience, watching the whole scene from the spectator's point of view, and he is also dimly conscious of the original and controlling Idea, which does not take the stage into account at all, but accepts or rejects every word according to some eternal scheme of values that is concerned only with the reality of all experience.

It is extremely difficult to make this trinity of awareness and this manifold incarnation of activity clear to those who have not experienced it; but if I have succeeded in interpreting the mind of the maker at all, the reader will see how impossible it is to say that the author is fully expressed in any speech, character, or single work of his. One must first put all these together and relate them to a great synthesis of all the work, which will be found to possess a unity of its own, to which every separate work is ultimately related. If we stop here, we have arrived at a pantheistic doctrine of the creative mind. But beyond that, the sum of all the work is related to the mind itself, which made it, controls it, and relates it to its own creative personality. The mind is not the sum of its works, though it includes them all. Though it produced the works one after the other, we cannot say that it *is* each of these works in turn. Before it made them, it included them all, potentially, and having finished them, it still includes them. It is both immanent in them and transcendent.

It will not, however, do to go further and say that the works themselves have no reality apart from the author's mind. Although his personality includes them all, and although there is nothing in them that is not also in him, yet, as soon as they are expressed in material form they have a separate reality *for us*. And not only a material reality—that is, we are aware of them not merely as a certain weight and outline of printed paper, but as individualities, exercising as much influence upon us as our own individualities exercise on one another. We can be aware of them without any direct awareness of the author: to put it crudely, we may, and do, know the *Iliad* without knowing Homer.

That fact does not prevent our being eager to know the author by direct awareness. Homer is out of our reach, and Shakespeare also is a *deus absconditus*, though we do our inquisitive best to establish contact with him behind and beyond his work as well as within it. Our speculations about Shakespeare are almost as multifarious and foolish as our speculations about the maker of the universe, and, like those, are frequently concerned to establish that his works were not made by him but by another person of the same name. The itch for personally knowing authors torments most of us; we feel that if we could somehow get at the man himself, we should obtain more help and satisfaction from him than from his chosen self-revelation. In certain cases, indeed, we may effect this and establish a real personal contact, but the world of literary appreciation cannot, any more than the world of religion, be populated by pure contemplatives only. And it is desirable to bear in mind—when dealing with the human maker at any rate—that his chosen way of revelation *is* through his works. To persist in asking, as so many of us do, "What did you mean by this book?" is to invite bafflement: the book itself is what the writer means. It is hopeless to expect, that is, that we can ever be made directly aware of the Idea— the writer himself is not aware of it except through the Energy and all he can communicate to us is the Energy made manifest in Power.

I have spoken from time to time of the author's books as "finished" works. With the human author working with his finite mind inside the limits of time and space, it is, of course, possible for us to look from time to time upon a work that is finished. In the narrower sense, each separate book is a thing completed; in a rather wider sense, we can say, at the end of the writer's life, that our bookshelf contains his "Complete Works." This privilege is ours because we belong to the same category of being as the writer, so that the memory of the human race includes the whole span of his activity.

When we apply the analogy to the work of the divine Creator, we cannot look at things in quite this way. We consider God as a living author, whose span of activity extends infinitely beyond our racial memory in both directions. We never see His great work finished. Here and there we seem to recognize something which looks like the end of a chapter or the last page of a volume; or an episode presents itself to us as having a kind of completeness and unity in itself. There is, indeed, a school of thought which imagines that God, having created His universe, has now screwed the cap on His pen, put up His feet on the mantelpiece and left the work to get on with itself. This, however, rather comes into St. Augustine's category of figures of speech or enigmatic sayings framed from things which do not exist at all. We simply do not know of any creation which goes on creating itself in variety when the creator has withdrawn from it. The idea is that God simply created a vast machine and has left it working till it runs down for lack of fuel. This is another of those obscure analogies, since we have no experience of machines that produce variety of their own accord: the nature of a machine is to do the same thing over and over again so long as it keeps going. We may perhaps allow the analogy some force if we conceive of the machine as a kind of kaleidoscope, which mechanically shuffles all the physical units of the universe until all the permutations and combinations have been gone through; but this analogy fails to account for the results of human creativeness. If true, it means that not only must the material form of Cervantes be destroyed to produce the material form of Charles Dickens, but that the spiritual form of Don Quixote must be destroyed to produce the spiritual form of Mr. Pickwick. This, as we have already reminded ourselves, is not the case. The conclusion would seem to be that Don Quixote and Mr. Pickwick are not of this world at all: a theory which is perfectly arguable but which does not come within the ambit of the kaleidoscope-metaphor. We will therefore stick to the analogy which we have chosen—that of the imaginative creator—and continue with it, keeping very clearly in view the limitation that it applies to the living artist, engaged in a creative act, of which we cannot yet see the finished results.

We are thus considering the temporal universe as one of those great serial works of which installments appear from time to time, all related to a central idea whose completeness is not yet manifest to the reader. Within the framework of its diversity are many minor and partial unities—of plot, of episode, and of character. By our response to it, we are brought within the mind of the author and are caught up into the stream of his Power, which proceeds from his Energy, revealing his Idea to us and to himself.

V

FREE WILL AND MIRACLE

God created man in his own image and likeness, i.e. made him a creator too, calling him to free spontaneous activity and not to formal obedience to His power. Free creativeness is the creature's answer to the great call of its creator. Man's creative work is the fulfilment of the Creator's secret will. —BERDYAEV: *The Destiny of Man*

A character in a writer's head, unwritten, remains a possession; his thoughts recur to it constantly, and while his imagination gradually enriches it he enjoys the singular pleasure of feeling that there, in his mind, someone is living a varied and tremulous life, obedient to his fancy and yet in a queer, wilful way independent of him. —W. SOMERSET MAUGHAM: *Preface to "Cakes and Ale"*

FREE WILL AND MIRACLE

IN considering the question how far the writer should permit his imagined characters to become the mouthpieces of his personality, we touched the fringe of that permanently baffling problem, the free will of the creature. All characters, from the most important to the least, and from the best to the worst, must express some part of the maker's mind if they are to be a living creation; but if all express that mind in an identical way, the work as a whole becomes dull, mechanical, and untrue. At this point we begin to see faintly the necessity for some kind of free will among the creatures of a perfect creation, but our metaphor now becomes very difficult to apply, since it appears obvious that the characters invented by a human writer are his helpless puppets, bound to obey his will at every point, whether for good or evil.

The analogy of procreation is more helpful to us here than that of artistic creation. While the parent is wholly responsible for calling the children into being, and can exercise a partial control over their minds and actions, he cannot but recognize the essential independence of the entity that he has procreated. The child's will is perfectly free; if he obeys his father, he does so through love or fear or respect, but not as an automaton, and the good parent would not wish it otherwise. We may observe here one of those curious complexities of which

63

human nature is full. There is in many parents a striving to control their children, and to make of them, if not precisely automata, yet beings as fully subordinate to the will of their procreator as the characters of a novelist are to their creator. On the other hand, there is in the human creator a parallel desire to create something that shall have as much free will as the offspring of procreation. The stories which tell of attempts to manufacture robots and Frankenstein monsters bear witness to this strange desire. It is as though humanity were conscious of a hampering limitation of its functions; in man, the image of the divine strives, as it were, to resemble its original in both its creative and procreative functions: to be at once father and God. From experience I am inclined to think that one reason why writing for the stage is so much more interesting than writing for publication is the very fact that, when the play is acted, the free will of the actor is incorporated into the written character. The common man is aware of the conflicting desires within the playwright's mind, and often asks questions about them. Sometimes he asks: "Isn't it exciting to see your characters come alive upon the stage?" Sometimes he inquires sympathetically: "Isn't it maddening to hear the actors ruining your best lines?" The playwright can only reply that (unless the production is quite unnaturally good or superlatively bad) both propositions are undoubtedly true.[1]

A good deal, of course, depends upon the temperament of the playwright. If he is of the egotistical kind, finding no satisfaction except in the autocratic enforce-

[1] See Chapter X, *subt.*

ment of his sole will, he will find actors maddening almost beyond endurance. This is the type of person who, in the sphere of procreation, tends to become a Roman parent. But if he is the more liberal kind of creator, he will eagerly welcome—I will not say bad acting, which is altogether sinful and regrettable—but imaginative and free acting, and find an immensely increased satisfaction in the individual creativeness which the actor brings to his part. And let it be said at once that if the part is well conceived and well written, good acting, however free and individual, can never harm it. The greater the part, the greater the variety of "good" interpretations: that is why (contrary to lay belief) it is much easier to play "Hamlet" in *Hamlet* than to play "Charles, his friend" in a third-rate sentimental comedy. To hear an intelligent and sympathetic actor infusing one's own lines with his creative individuality is one of the most profound satisfactions that any imaginative writer can enjoy; more —there is an intimately moving delight in watching the actor's mind at work to deal rightly with a difficult interpretation, for there is in all this a joy of communication and an exchange of power. Within the limits of this human experience, the playwright has achieved that complex end of man's desire—the creation of a living thing with a mind and will of its own.

None of this delight will, however, be gained unless the playwright is devoured with a real love for material form—unless, in the writing of the play, his Energy has imaginatively moved upon the stage in the way I have tried to explain, and conceived its Idea in material terms of flesh and blood, and paint, and canvas. For the true freedom of the Energy consists in its willing submission to the limitations of its own medium. The attempt to achieve freedom *from* the medium ends inevitably in loss of freedom *within* the medium, since, here as everywhere, activity falls under the judgment of the law of its own nature. Take, for example, that kind of writing for the stage which is called—with damnatory intent—"literary" drama. The objection to it is not that it is (in the broad sense) "literature," but that it is so written as to conform to an alien literary medium. The speeches are quite simply not constructed in such a way as to be readily spoken by an actor. This means that the writer's Energy has arrogated to itself a freedom from natural law—it has refused to be bound by the trammels imposed by flesh and blood. The immediate consequence of this freedom is an intolerable sense of restriction, and the verdict of the critic will be that "the language is labored." The truth is that such speech is not "labored" enough—in the sense that it has not been given enough workmanship. Similar efforts towards an illegal freedom issue in unmanageable stage-directions, or a multiplicity of vast stage-sets, which no amount of engineering effort can hurry upon the stage swiftly enough to preserve the unities. The business of the creator is not to escape from his material medium or to bully it, but to serve it; but to serve it he must love it. If he does so, he will realize that its service is perfect freedom. This is true, not only of all literary art but of all creative art; I have chosen a theatrical example, merely because there, as also in the creation of characters, failure to surrender to the law of kind produces disasters more patent and immediate than elsewhere.

The judgment of the natural law is not without its

bearing on the writer's claim to autocratic control over the characters he invents. It is certainly true that these do not possess free will to the same extent that a child's will is free from parental control. But all possess this measure of freedom, namely, that unless the author permits them to develop in conformity with their proper nature, they will cease to be true and living creatures.

Too much attention should not be paid to those writers who say (holding one the while with a fixed and hypnotic gaze): "I don't really invent the plot, you know—I just let the characters come into my mind and let them take charge of it." The theory that the mind can remain passive and empty, acting only as a kind of automatic "spirit-hand" for the characters, reminds one a little too much of the methods of "Savonarola Brown" and his gasping confidences: "Savonarola has come on—*alive!*" [2] Writers who work in this way do not, as a matter of brutal fact, usually produce very good books. The lay public (most of them confirmed mystagogues) rather like to believe in this inspirational fancy; but as a rule the element of pure craftsmanship is more important than most of us are willing to admit.

Nevertheless, the free will of a genuinely created character has a certain reality, which the writer will defy at his peril. It does sometimes happen that the plot requires from its characters certain behavior, which, when it comes to the point, no ingenuity on the author's part can force them into, except at the cost of destroying them. It may be that the Activity has chosen an unsuitable plot, or (this is perhaps more frequent) has imagined an

[2] Max Beerbohm: *Seven Men.*

unsuitable set of characters for working that particular plot out.

In such dilemmas, the simplest and worst thing the author can do is to behave like an autocratic deity and compel the characters to do his will whether or not. Theurgic exhibitions of this kind are frequent in the work of thriller-writers and in the more puerile type of film. A notorious instance is, of course, that open-hearted and generous-minded young lover whom we so frequently see thrown into consternation by the discovery of his betrothed embracing a total stranger in the conservatory. If the lover were to behave in conformity with his character as laid down for him, he would trust the girl and await the very obvious and proper explanation, *viz.*, that the stranger is her long-lost brother suddenly returned home. But since any such natural conduct would bring the story to a premature end, he is forced to deny his nature, believe the worst, and depart hot-foot for a distant country.

This hoary piece of untruth does little harm to the nonsensical fancies in which it is usually found embedded, since these are not, in any genuine sense, works of creative imagination. It is startling, however, to find a variation of it violently intruded into the last act of such an otherwise realistically conceived and honestly written play as Denys Amiel's *Famille*.[3] Here its effect is disastrous, for the characters have a true nature to be destroyed; and the collapse of the power is in direct ratio to the previous strength of the characterization.

Similar, though rather more subtle, wrestings of natu-

[3] First produced in Paris, 1937.

ral truth abound in those romances where the heroine,
after treating the hero for interminable chapters as
though he were something the cat had brought in, is rescued by him under peculiarly humiliating circumstances
and immediately falls into his arms in a passion of gratitude and affection. Knowledge of the very ephemeral
nature of gratitude in proud and vain persons and of its
irritating effect on the character, prompt the reader to
wonder what the married life of the couple is likely to
be, after thus starting from a false situation. It is a falsity
of this kind that makes both actors and audience uncom-
fortable about *The Taming of the Shrew;* whether it is
played as burlesque or softened into sentimental comedy, we are still left protesting that " 'Tis a wonder, by
your leave, she will be tamed so," and nothing will persuade us that characters like those would really subdue
themselves to a plot like that.

Yet another forcible deformation of natural character
occurs when the author has allowed a character to develop along its natural lines without noticing that it has
grown right away from the part it is called on to play in
the plot. Mr. Micawber is a grand character, instinct
with the breath of life; but inefficiency is of his very
essence, and it is entirely inconceivable that he should
ever have become an efficient detective for the investigation of Mr. Heep's financial frauds. *Somebody* had to
detect Heep, and Mr. Micawber was handy—may indeed
have been designed from the outset—for the activity;
but, superb fun though it all is, we cannot for one moment believe it.

The humanistic and sensitive author may prefer to
take the course of sticking to his characters and altering

the plot to suit their development. This will result in a less violent shock to the reader's sense of reality, but also in an alarming incoherence of structure. Actions adumbrated at the beginning will fail to materialize; causes will be left without consequences, or with irrational consequences; the balance of the unity will be upset; and the book will trail away into disorder, or, in the critic's picturesque phrase, "break its back." At the worst, the theme (or bodily shape of the Idea) will disappear along with the plot. The reader will probably not be able to put his finger with any great certainty on the point at which the book goes wrong, but he will be left at the end with an instinctive awareness that there is a dislocation somewhere. So will the author. In extreme cases, the dislocation will be so shattering as to prevent the book from ever getting written. A most instructive account of how the unbridled development of free will in the characters wrecked the prospects of a work of imagination is given by J. D. Beresford in that extraordinarily fascinating book: *Writing Aloud*. Here, with a candor and accuracy extremely rare in a writer, he traces the development of—or failure to develop—a theme which he tried for some years to embody in a novel, and which eventually defeated him because of the self-willed behavior of the characters. As the story shapes itself in his mind, the plot dislimns, reunites in new shapes; the center of interest shifts from one character to another, and we watch, with spell-bound apprehension (if we are framed to feel excitement about such matters) the foredoomed metamorphosis of the theme into something like its own direct opposite. It is as though we watched an army outflanked and pivoting to face an attack that moves gradually round to attack it from the rear. Beresford himself believes that the discrepancies in the story

illustrate Mr. Forster's remarks on the relation of character to plot; inasmuch as they show very plainly that when plot precedes character and must be adhered to whatever happens, character inevitably suffers.

His book itself, however, shows still more plainly that the trouble is not so simple as all that. What preceded plot and everything else was the fancy for presenting the character of a particular heroine.

I should like her to be young next time; very young; and pre-war. . . . A pre-war heroine living in the present day. . . . She represents the "average woman" that is eternal throughout the ages. She shall be neither tall nor short, neither very dark nor very fair, neither alluringly beautiful nor noticeably plain, neither too clever nor a fool, neither hopelessly womanly (the "perfect wife and mother" sort of thing) nor the kind we have read about so much lately [1927] who devotes herself to some art or profession, and babbles about woman's freedom. She shall play games in moderation without making a fetish of them. She is original by not striving after originality, and with any luck I may achieve the same ideal, myself. If one could but make a convincing picture of the ordinary human girl, how she would show up against the young woman we get so much of now, in life and fiction.

With that character he begins—not, we may note, with a character in a situation, but a character looking for a situation to exploit. The story is then gradually built up —background, plot, parentage and so forth—deliberately in order to account for and exploit the character of this girl (nicknamed, "J-J"). Other characters—arising this time out of the plot—supervene, and in turn arrogate to themselves the greater part of the writer's creative interest. Being plot-founded (conceived, that is, as characters *in* a situation) they are enormously more powerful than the detached character of J-J; already the attackers have captured the "strong points." Thus firmly based and equipped, they grow and cover the ground with the speed and ubiquity of pumpkins, and subdue the situation to their own will; they take command of the plot. After a hundred pages or so of this development the author stands aghast:

> In this book, struggle as I will, I do not seem to be able to stick to my first intention of telling the story of J-J. She, poor lamb, has so far served me only as a vaulting-horse, she who was to have been my ideal heroine, my interpreter. Instead of presenting a model for the girl of 1930 or so, she has become a horrible instance of Victorian repressions, a subject for vivisection, a manikin for the display of other people's habits, anything in short but an interesting human being.

For this disaster he can find no remedy. Either he must scrap the whole thing, or else "keep the other characters and the skeleton of the plot, but bravely sacrifice all the development I have so far worked out, get a truer understanding of my heroine and let her personality guide the evolution of the story. That would mean cutting out all the things that really interested myself." What did in fact interest him was "the other characters"; there is actually no plot except what those characters have themselves imposed on the story. The impasse was complete, and the story was eventually scrapped, except in so far as it provides the subject for this revealing work of analysis.

Anybody who reads *Writing Aloud* will find entertainment in discovering how it was that the "other characters," rather than J-J, contrived in this manner to run away with the plot. The thing that emerges very clearly is a disruption within the writer's trinity: his Energy was not subdued to the Idea—or else merely revealed in its working the absence of any really powerful idea to control it—and the consequence is a judgment of chaos.

We will now look at another instructive example of "back-breaking" which Chesterton has observed in *Our Mutual Friend:*

> If the real degradation of Wegg is not very convincing, it is at least immeasurably more convincing than the pretended degradation of Boffin. The passage in which Boffin appears as a sort of miser, and then afterwards explains that he only assumed the character for reasons of his own, has something about it highly jerky and unsatisfactory. The truth of the whole matter, I think, almost certainly, is that Dickens did not originally mean Boffin's lapse to be fictitious. He originally meant Boffin really to be corrupted by wealth, slowly to degenerate and as slowly to repent. But the story went too quickly for this long, double, and difficult process; therefore Dickens at the last moment made a sudden recovery possible by representing that the whole business had been a trick. Consequently, this episode is not an error merely in the sense that we may find many errors in a great writer like Dickens; it is a mistake patched up with another mistake. It is a case of that ossification which occurs round the healing of an actual fracture; the story had broken down and been mended.[4]

[4] G. K. Chesterton: *Criticisms and Appreciations of the Works of Charles Dickens.*

What happened (if Chesterton is right, as I think he is [5]) was that Dickens "fell in love" with Boffin, with the result that the character "got out of hand" or, in other words, asserted the freedom of its nature. This kind of thing does happen to characters from time to time—never, of course, to the puppet-character, but only to those that have received a full measure of the author's life—and their escape from control is the measure of their free will. What is particularly interesting here is the method adopted by Dickens to bring plot and character back into co-operation. He took what should have been the right way out of the difficulty, but so clumsily that the result was unconvincing and false.

The character of Boffin had asserted itself to a point at which it literally *could not* be made to conform with the plot. I doubt whether the speed at which the story was moving accounts sufficiently for the impossibility; what really stood in the way was the intrinsic sweetness and modesty of Mr. Boffin himself. A means had there-

[5] Dickens was perfectly capable of such a change of purpose. He writes to Forster, while engaged on *Dombey & Son:* "About the boy [Walter Gay] . . . I think it would be a good thing to disappoint all the expectations that chapter seems to raise of his happy connection with the story and the heroine, and to show him gradually and naturally trailing away, from that love of adventure and boyish light-heartedness, into negligence, idleness, dissipation, dishonesty and ruin. To show, in short, that common, every-day, miserable declension of which we know so much in our ordinary life, to exhibit something of the philosophy of it, in great temptations and an easy nature; and to show how the good turns into bad, by degrees. . . . Do you think it may be done, without making people angry?" For reasons which Forster does not specify, but which may be guessed, Walter Gay was spared, and the picture of "great temptations and an easy nature" postponed till the appearance of Richard Carstairs in *Bleak House;* but the author's indecisions have left their mark on *Dombey* in Walter's oddly haphazard connection with the plot-structure.

fore to be found by which the character, developing in conformity with its own nature, could yet bring the plot to the same issue which it would have reached had the character developed according to plan.

The process which I shall now try to explain is something for which the reader must take my word. I cannot easily point to any successful examples in literature, because it is the whole essence of such a process that, if it is successful, nothing in the finished work will betray it. I can only state, as matter of experience, that if the characters and the situation are rightly conceived together, as integral parts of the same unity, then there will be no need to force them to the right solution of that situation. If each is allowed to develop in conformity with its proper nature, all will arrive of their own accord at a point of unity, which will be the same unity that pre-existed in the original idea. In language to which we are accustomed in other connections, neither predestination nor free will is everything, but, if the will acts freely in accordance with its true nature, it achieves by grace and not by judgment the eternal will of its maker, though possibly by a process unlike, and longer than, that which might have been imposed upon it by force.

As I have said, it is hard to illustrate this from other men's work, since, when it has triumphantly happened, the process leaves no trace, and the majority of writers have not left analytical records of their creative activities. I tried once [6] to analyze a very unimportant experience of my own in this connection—unimportant, that is, because the work itself was of no great importance ex-

[6] See my essay in *Titles to Fame*.

cept to myself. Here, I will only bring forward an instance, also personally experienced but still more trivial, of this odd coming-together of plot and character. This instance is, in a way, more interesting than the other, because the process occurred without my being at all aware of it, so that I was astonished when I saw the result.

In *Gaudy Night*, the heroine was left in one of those "gratitude-situations" which (as I have already complained) are so destructive to character and leave the normal person so little disposed to fall into the arms of the benefactor. She had, however, been brought into a fair way of conquering her pride (assisted by a similar approach from the gentleman's side) and had screwed herself to the point of making a generous gesture and accepting a present from him. The present selected was a set of carved ivory chessmen. In all this, the characters were working out their own development without reference to anything beyond their own spiritual difficulties.

In the meantime, the detective-plot situation was concerned with a woman in whom the emotions had gained control over the reason, and who was carrying on a revenge-campaign of petty destructiveness against certain women who (she felt) were sacrificing the emotional to the rational. Her anger had directed itself against my heroine, with the result that she (and I) were left looking for something belonging to the heroine that she might conveniently destroy. It then occurred to me that the chessmen were the obvious victims; their destruction duly took place, and revealed to the heroine that some of her value for them was connected, not with the gift but with the giver.

A reader afterwards said to me: "I realized, the moment they were mentioned, that those chessmen were doomed." Nothing, when one comes to think of it, could be more obvious from the point of view of plot-structure. I can only affirm (without much hope of being believed) that it was by no means obvious to *me*. The chessmen were, at first, connected with the character-development, and with that only. But when the plot demanded their destruction, there they were ready. Though I did at that moment realize that this incident clamped the two parts of the story together in a satisfactory and useful manner, it was not until my reader pointed it out to me that I understood the incident to have been, in actual fact, predestined—that is, that plot and character, each running true to its nature, had inevitably united to bring the thing about.

I could add a further example of the same kind of thing. In *Murder Must Advertise* I undertook (not very successfully) to present a contrast of two "cardboard" worlds, equally fictitious—the world of advertising and the world of the post-war "Bright Young People." (It was not very successful, because I knew and cared much more about advertising than about Bright Youth, but that is by the way.) I mentioned this intention to a reader, who instantly replied: "Yes; and Peter Wimsey, who represents reality, never appears in either world except in disguise." It was perfectly true; and I had never noticed it. With all its defects of realism, there had been some measure of integral truth about the book's Idea, since it issued, without my conscious connivance, in a true symbolism.

Other writers will probably be able to supply evidence of their own in support of this curious collaboration of free will and predestination wherever plot and character are allowed to develop in obedience to their law of nature. And these considerations bring us face to face with the whole question of miracle.

Whatever we may think of the possibilities of direct divine intervention in the affairs of the universe, it is quite evident that the writer can—and often does—intervene at any moment in the development of his own story; he is absolute master, able to perform any miracle he likes. I do not mean that he can invent undiscovered planets or people the world with monsters unknown to natural history—that kind of thing is a tale about marvels, not a tale abruptly modified by marvels. I mean simply that he can twist either character or plot from the course of its nature by an exertion of arbitrary power. He can slay inconvenient characters, effect abrupt conversions, or bring about accidents or convulsions of nature to rescue the characters from the consequences of their own conduct. He can, in fact, behave exactly as, in our more egotistical and unenlightened petitions, we try to persuade God to behave. Whether we mock at miracles or demand miracles, this is the kind of miracle we usually mean. We mean that the judgment of natural law is to be abrogated by some power extraneous to the persons and circumstances.

If we by analogy call God "the Creator" we are thereby admitting that it is *possible* for Him to work miracles; but if we examine more closely the implications of our analogy, we may be driven to ask ourselves how far it is really *desirable* that He should do anything of the kind. For the example of the writers who indulge in miracle is not altogether encouraging. "Poetic justice" (the name often given to artistic miracle-mongering) may be comforting, but we regretfully recognize that it is very bad art. "Poetic justice" is indeed the wrong name to give it, since it is neither poetry nor justice; there is a true poetic justice, which we know better by the name of "tragic irony," which is of the nature of judgment and is the most tremendous power in literature as in life—but in that there is no element of miracle. What we commonly mean by "poetic justice" is a system of rewards and punishments bestowed, like their nursery exemplars, "because you have been good" and "because you have been naughty"—or sometimes simply with the object of keeping the children quiet.

Mr. Wilkins Micawber—who is continually the subject of such theurgic displays—is favored by a miracle at the end of *David Copperfield*. He is a "good" character—that is to say, a character sympathetic to his author—and it is desired to reward him with a "happy ending." He is therefore packed off to Australia, where, in defiance of his own nature and in defiance of the nature of Australian civic life in the last century, he becomes a prosperous magistrate. However consoling this solution of the Micawber problem, a little thought convinces us that any person less suitable to prosper in these conditions than Mr. Micawber can scarcely be imagined. It is miracle; just as the sudden appearance of a couple of aged and worthy parents to straighten out lovers' difficulties in the last act of Molière's *L'Ecole des Femmes* is miracle. The author, finding that plot and character will not work within their own limitations to produce a tidy result, has cut the Gordian entanglement with the magic sword of Paracelsus. The result is not only to shock us with a sense of incongruity, but also to detract something from the power of Micawber himself. He is so much the less a man for being the minion of so arbitrary a favoritism.

Wilkie Collins, a much lesser writer than Dickens, dealing with a similar problem, shows himself a much more conscientious artist. At the end of *No Name* he has to dispose of the unscrupulous but strongly sympathetic out-at-elbows scamp, Captain Wragge. He might have worked a moral miracle, by making the Captain repent and live happily in honest poverty; or a physical miracle, by unexpectedly endowing him with a colossal fortune which should remove the need for further rogueries. Either of these methods would destroy the Captain as we know him. Collins does artistically better, by providing him with a way to prosperity fully in accordance with his character:

"What have I been about? Why do I look so remarkably well off? . . . My dear girl, I have been occupied, since we last saw each other, in slightly modifying my old professional habits. . . . Formerly I preyed on the public sympathy; now, I prey on the public stomach. . . . Here I am—incredible as it may appear—a man with an income, at last. The founders of my fortune are three in number. Their names are Aloes, Scammony and Gamboge. In plainer words, I am now living—on a Pill. I made a little money (if you remember) by my friendly connection with you. I made a little more, by the happy decease (Requiescat in Pace!) of that female relative of Mrs. Wragge's, from whom, as I told you, my wife had expectations. Very good.

What do you think I did? I invested the whole of my capital, at one fell swoop, in advertisements—and purchased my drugs and my pill-boxes on credit. The result is now before you."

Here is a happy peripety which we can readily accept. We can believe in the profits of roguery; we can believe in the little legacy (since we were previously told that he married his half-witted wife to obtain it); and we can believe in these acquisitions all the better because, undoubtedly, this is the very way in which Captain Wragge would use them if he got them. It is a happy ending for a sympathetic rascal, which satisfies us because it is no miracle but a judgment of natural law.

But it is not edifying? Well, no, it is not. The making of miracles to edification was as ardently admired by pious Victorians as it was sternly discouraged by Jesus of Nazareth. Not that the Victorians are unique in this respect. Modern writers also indulge in edifying miracles though they generally prefer to use them to procure unhappy endings, by which piece of thaumaturgy they win the title of realists. Thus, in Cronin's *The Citadel* it is necessary to edification that his doctor-hero shall be stripped of every personal satisfaction—wealth, reputation, and domestic happiness—in order that he may voluntarily embrace the good he once refused, namely, medical research for unselfish ends. This is right enough, from the point of view of religion and psychology. Of wealth and reputation he is deprived, very properly, by a judgment of natural law, executing itself upon his own professional conduct. But when it comes to his domestic happiness, the author grows impatient. He has already prepared estrangement between husband and wife through the doctor's behavior; but for no very adequate reason, he suddenly abandons this line of development, and by an arbitrary act, hastily gets rid of the wife by pushing her under a bus. One cannot defend this intervention by saying that virtuous people in real life are frequently killed by road-vehicles. The episode is wholly extraneous to the structural unity of the story; it is an irrelevant miracle. The effect is to falsify the story. The divine hand is thrust into the mechanism obviously and without necessity: *nec deus intersit nisi dignus vindice nodus.*[7]

The agents of the miraculous which the novelist has at his command are, roughly speaking, conversion and coincidence; either a character or a situation is abruptly changed, not by anything developing out of the essentials of the story, but by the personal divine intervention of the creator. Yet it will not altogether do to say that neither conversion nor coincidence is *ever* permissible in a story. Both may legitimately be introduced on one condition, that is, that they are an integral part of the Idea. If it is a story *about* a coincidence or *about* a conversion, then the Energy that introduces them will be performing the will of the Idea, and the Power will proceed from that unity of purpose. This amounts to saying that, under these circumstances, the will of the creator becomes a character in the story; just as, theologically, all miracles depend on the assumption that God is a character in history. But even so, it is necessary that God should act in conformity with His own character. The study of our analogy will lead us perhaps to believe that

[7] "Nor let God intervene unless the difficulty be worthy of his attention."—EDITOR'S NOTE.

God will be chary of indulging in irrelevant miracle, and will use it only when it is an integral part of the story. He will not, any more than a good writer, convert His characters without preparing the way for their conversion, and His interferences with space-time will be conditioned by some kind of relationship of power between will and matter. Faith is the condition for the removal of mountains; Lear is converted but not Iago. Consequences cannot be separated from their causes without a loss of power; and we may ask ourselves how much power would be left in the story of the crucifixion, as a story, if Christ had come down from the cross. That would have been an irrelevant miracle, whereas the story of the resurrection is relevant, leaving the consequences of action and character still in logical connection with their causes. It is, in fact, an outstanding example of the development we have already considered—the leading of the story back, by the new and more powerful way of grace, to the issue demanded by the way of judgment, so that the law of nature is not destroyed but fulfilled.

VI

THE ENERGY INCARNATE IN SELF-EXPRESSION

Then came, at a predetermined moment, a moment in time and out of time,

A moment not out of time, but in time, in what we call history; transecting, bisecting the world of time, a moment in time but not like a moment of time,

A moment in time, but time was made through that moment: for without the meaning there is no time, and that moment of time gave the meaning. —T. S. ELIOT: *The Rock*

THE ENERGY INCARNATE IN SELF-EXPRESSION

THE mind of the maker is generally revealed, and in a manner incarnate, in all its creation. The works, severally and jointly, are manifestations within space-time of the Energy and instinct with the Power of the Idea. Thus the Spirit of God brooded upon the face of the primeval waters and (says St. Irenaeus) "was present from everlasting with the race of men." The personality of the creator is expressed partially, piecemeal, and as it were impersonally or through created persons.

Christian doctrine further affirms that the Mind of the Maker was also incarnate personally and uniquely. Examining our analogy for something to which this may correspond, we may say that God wrote His own autobiography.

Clearly, we cannot press this analogy too far. But we may use it—as we have used all our analogies so far—to assist us in finding out what is *meant* by some of the more dark and difficult expressions used about this doctrine.

The Idea, in this connection, will be the full personality of the writer, and the Power will be the power of that personality. The Energy (in its discarnate aspect) will be his complete self-awareness of his own personality. This is, of course, a condition which no human writer can possibly fulfill, but for our purposes we shall have to suppose it, as we suppose the ideal parent and the ideal creative imagination. The Energy, being thus aware of the Idea of itself, manifests its Power in material form: that is to say, it creates for itself an intellectual form and material body.

The first thing we have to notice about this is that the body is created exactly like all the rest of the author's creations and suffers exactly the same limitations. The autobiography is a book like any other; all the ordinary rules of composition apply to it. It is unique, because the author appears, personally and without disguise, as a character in his own story; but it is still a story that he is writing, and he is obliged to handle his own character *as* a character throughout the succession of events. To himself, the character partakes of the eternal wholeness of his own personal awareness, but to the other characters and the reader it is presented within the space-time-matter frame of the book itself. It is the creator of that frame, since it arranges the formal presentation of the subject-matter, and at the same time it is completely submissive to the frame it has created. It appears with a double nature, "divine and human"; the whole story is contained within the mind of its maker, but the mind of the maker is also imprisoned within the story and cannot escape from it. It is "altogether God," in that it is sole arbiter of the form the story is to take, and yet "altogether man," in that, having created the form,[1] it is

---

[1] I do not, of course, suggest that the writer can create the space-time-matter *events* of his own life-history. The creative power of the human maker is, as we have seen, limited to the creation of significant form and of immaterial entities. It is within this framework of form and imagination that the autobiographical "I" has to conform with the law of its creation.

bound to display itself in conformity with the nature of that form.

A second point to notice is this: that the autobiography is at one and the same time a single element in the series of the writer's created works and an interpretation of the whole series. If we want (as so many of us do) to find out what the writer "means" by his writings, we shall undoubtedly get some light on the matter by reading his personal revelation of himself. If it is a good autobiography (and by hypothesis we are discussing the perfect autobiography) it will reveal to us the relation of all the other books to their author's Idea of himself, whether in likeness or unlikeness. It will do so, not only for the books written earlier, and not only in relation to the manifestation in time of the writer's Energy, but also in relation to the timeless Idea that is his personality. We shall be able to trace both his development in his life and works, and also the permanent identity of himself which transcends his development and which constitutes the thing we call his "*persona*." The exact place and moment, within the series of his works, for the appearance of the autobiography is selected at will by the writer, for reasons which he may or may not choose to explain; but at whatever point it comes, the revelation is valid, both for the past and for the future.

The personal revelation is unique: a writer cannot give us two autobiographies—that is, he cannot display himself as two persons with two different lives; any further revelations will be by the way of imaginative creation. Nor, since all human minds are bound by the conditions of humanity, can he very well reveal himself except under human form. If he could do so, the revelation would be of little interest to his readers, since they would not be able to understand it. There is, of course, no reason why an infinite Mind should not reveal itself in an infinite number of forms, each being subject to the nature of that particular form. It was said, sneeringly, by someone that if a clam could conceive of God, it would conceive of Him in the shape of a great, big clam. Naturally. And if God has revealed Himself to clams, it could be only under conditions of perfect clamhood, since any other manifestation would be wholly irrelevant to clam nature. By incarnation, the creator says in effect: "See! this is what my eternal Idea looks like in terms of my own creation; this is my manhood, this is my clamhood, this is my characterhood in a volume of created characters."

Thirdly: though the autobiography "is" the author in a sense in which his other works are not, it can never be the whole of the author. It is still a formal expression and bound by the limitations of all material form, so that though it is a true revelation it is only a partial revelation: it incorporates only so much of the mind as matter is capable of containing. Its incompleteness is not due to any imperfection in the mind; it is simply and solely due to the necessary limitations of literary form. Theologically, the Word is said to be "equal to the Father as touching His Godhead and inferior to the Father as touching His manhood"—which may be translated into the language of our analogy: "Equal to the Idea as touching its essence and inferior to the Idea as touching its expression." It is inferior, not only in the sense that it is limited by form as the Idea is not, but also in the sense that its form is creaturely and therefore subject to the

Idea—"I do the will of My Father." This does not mean that the revelation is not perfect; it is, as the phrase goes, "perfect of its kind"; but the kind itself is capable only of so much and no more.

There is a fourth point about the writing of autobiography which may be meditated on with profit (and some uneasiness) by the human creator. Like the creation of imagined character, but in a much higher degree, it is an infallible self-betrayal. The truth about the writer's personality will out, in spite of itself; any illusions which he may entertain about himself become fearfully apparent the moment he begins to handle himself as a created character, subject to the nature of his own art. As in every other work of creation, insincerity issues in false art. Here again, I do not refer to those candid confessions of his own faults which the human writer (if he is honest) will make part of the created character; they are a part of his Idea, and therefore part of the perfection of the autobiography—they are "good" in art. (Moral "goodness" is a different matter.) When, for example, Benvenuto Cellini delightedly lays bare his own roqueries, we acknowledge the perfect "rightness" of his self-expression. If, however, the author either consciously or unconsciously tries to incarnate himself as something other than what he is, there will be a falseness in the artistic expression corresponding to the false relation between Energy and Idea, and the result, as always, will be a failure of Power. This, in Art, is the unalterable law of kind, from which the artist can by no means escape; the truth of what he says about himself is tested by the truth of the form in which he says it. By its truth—not by its elegance or accomplishment, though the more accomplished the form the more readily will it betray its own lack of truth. It will show itself untrue, not in the moral sense of telling lies, but in the structural sense, which is what the builder means by saying that a line is "out of true."

For this reason, no considerations of false reverence should prevent us from subjecting the incarnations of creators to the severest tests of examination. It is right that they should be pulled about and subjected to the most searching kind of inquiry. If the structure is truly knit, it will stand any strain, and prove its truth by its toughness. Pious worshipers, whether of mortal or immortal artists, do their deities little honor by treating their incarnations as something too sacred for rough handling; they only succeed in betraying a fear lest the structure should prove flimsy or false. But the writing of autobiography is a dangerous business; it is a mark either of great insensitiveness to danger or of an almost supernatural courage. Nobody but a god can pass unscathed through the searching ordeal of incarnation.

VII

MAKER OF ALL THINGS–MAKER OF ILL THINGS

FAUSTUS: *Who made thee?*
MEPHISTOPHELES: *God; as the light makes the shadow.*
FAUSTUS: *Is God, then, evil?*
MEPHISTOPHELES: *God is only light,*
And in the heart of the light no shadow standeth,
Nor can I dwell within the light of heaven
Where God is all.
FAUSTUS: *What art thou, Mephistopheles?*
MEPHISTOPHELES: *I am the price that all things pay for being,*
The shadow on the world, thrown by the world
Standing in its own light, which light God is.
—DOROTHY SAYERS: *The Devil to Pay.*

*It was . . . declared by Aquinas that it was of the nature
of God to know all possibilities, and to determine which
possibility should become fact. "God would not know good
things perfectly, unless He also knew evil things . . . for,
since evil is not of itself knowable, forasmuch as 'evil is the
privation of good' as Augustine says, therefore evil can
neither be defined nor known except by good." Things
which are not and never will be He knows "not by vision,"
as He does all things that are, or will be, "but by simple intelligence." It is therefore part of that knowledge that He
should understand good in its deprivation, the identity of
heaven in its opposite identity of hell, but without "appro-
bation," without calling it into being at all.*

*It was not so possible for man . . . To be as gods meant,
for the Adam, to die, for to know evil, for them, was to
know it not by pure intelligence but by experience.*
—CHARLES WILLIAMS: *He Came Down from Heaven*

MAKER OF ALL THINGS–MAKER OF
ILL THINGS

"IF God made everything, did He make the Devil?"

This is the kind of embarrassing question which any child can ask before breakfast, and for which no neat and handy formula is provided in the Parents' Manuals. In much the same light-hearted manner, a cousin of my own once demanded, "Mother, where has yesterday gone to?" My aunt courageously undertook to find out; but by the time she returned, primed with the opinion of an eminent Oxford philosopher, the inquirer had lost interest and, like jesting Pilate, would not stay for an answer.

Later in life, however, the problem of time and the problem of evil become desperately urgent, and it is useless to tell us to run away and play and that we shall understand when we are older. The world has grown hoary, and the questions are still unanswered.

The Manichaean [1] answer to the question about the Devil has the merit of appearing very sensible and of offering a reasonable explanation of the surface phenomena of this troubled world. The good God did not make evil and is not omnipotent. There are two principles in

[1] The Manichaeans were believers in the doctrines of Mani, or Manes, or Manichaeus, a Persian of the third century who taught that man's body is the product of the Kingdom of Darkness, but that his soul comes from the Kingdom of Light.—EDITOR'S NOTE.

the world, always at war, and more or less equally matched—God, equated with Light and Good; and the Archon, equated with Darkness and Matter. According to the myth, the powers of Darkness attacked the powers of Light, and carried away captive the Ray of Light or Ideal Man. God counter-attacked and set free the greater and better part of Man, but left the weaker part —the *Jesus patibilis*—enslaved to the Dark powers, who out of this part formed Mortal Man. "Thus Man was orginally formed in the image of Satan, but contained within him a spark of the heavenly light, which awaits its final deliverance by separation from the enveloping darkness." [2] According to this doctrine, matter (and therefore the body) is altogether evil,[3] and the victory of the good can be secured only by a strict asceticism. Sacramentalism can find no place in the religion of Mani. It will be noticed that the triumph of the Good is held to be finally assured; this seems to be a necessary assumption, or why should we call it Good? This doctrine accounts reasonably enough for the inextricable mingling of Good and Evil in Man, but not for the existence of Evil itself. The child may continue to ask, "Who made the Devil?" and also "Who made God, and how can we be sure that God will win in the end?"

Another theory is that Evil has no positive existence, but is only a deprivation of Good.[4] The Devil is a negation—*der Geist der stets verneint.*[5] This is confusing and

[2] *Chambers' Encyclopaedia:* Art: Manichaeus.
[3] Manichee doctrine admits the historical Jesus (*Jesus impatibilis*) but holds Him to have been no mortal man, but a phantasm, who did not really suffer in His body.
[4] St. Augustine: *Confessions,* iii. 7.
[5] The spirit that forever denies.—EDITOR'S NOTE.

difficult, but much more in harmony with Western feeling than the contrary theory of the Buddhists, that the supreme good is the attainment of Nothingness; the latter also leads to a wholly ascetic way of life and a condemnation of the material body.

Finally, there is the doctrine that the ultimate Godhead is neither good nor evil, but "beyond good and evil."

This is not the place in which to examine all these theories upon their merits. We may, however, see whether we can find in our literary analogy anything at all which may throw light on the nature of Evil.

Here again, we must issue a warning at the start. "Evil," for our purpose, must not be considered as being *moral evil*. The human maker, living and walking within a universe where Evil (whatever it is) is part of the nature of things, is obliged to take both Good and Evil as part of his Idea. They are the medium with which he works. We can consider only the special type of Evil which may make its appearance in connection with his particular act of creation—the type which is briefly summed up in the expression "bad art." In the choice of words, for example, the "right" word will not be the morally edifying word, but the word which "rightly" embodies his Idea, whether the Idea itself is morally good, evil, or "beyond good and evil." For him, engaged in his creative act, "good" is good craftsmanship, "beauty" is artistic beauty, and "truth" is structural truth. We must not, that is, confuse our minds by allowing our analogy to extrude itself outside its terms of reference.

We will also remember that we are not, for the moment, discussing what happens to a bad writer. A bad writer is so clearly the author of the badness in his books that the point scarcely needs making. If the Creator of the world is wicked, then we are not obliged to think up difficult answers to the question, "Who made the Devil?" The difficulty arises only when we say, "God made everything and God is good: then where did Evil come from?" Is there, then, within the terms of our analogy, any sense in which we can say that a good writer is the creator of artistic evil—or artistic "wrongness"?

It is here that we come up against a bunch of fascinating speculations about the "on kai me on"—being and not-being. It is all very well for Marlowe's Faustus to exclaim impatiently, "Bid oncaymeon farewell"—the inquisitive mind finds it very difficult to bid farewell to this intriguing subject. "Being" we can make a shift to understand, but what is "not-being"? If we propose to ourselves to "think about nothing," we find we have engaged in a very difficult exercise. It does not seem to be quite the same as "not thinking about anything." "Nothing" seems to remain nothing only as long as we refrain from thinking about it; any active thought is apt to turn it into a "sort of a something"—it acquires, in fact, precisely that vague and disquieting sort of reality that we are accustomed to associate with the minus signs in algebra. Professor Eddington has put the essentials of the problem neatly before us in the riddling query: "Is the bung-hole part of the barrel?" It depends, as he says, on what you mean by "part"; it may also depend, to some extent, on what you mean by the "barrel." This is where we get tied into knots over the definition of Evil as the "deprivation of Good"; we have to explain to ourselves why this wholly negative concept takes on the appearance of a very positive and active phenomenon.

"He created the world out of nothing"—nothing existed before it was made; that is, colloquially speaking, easy. It is less easy if it presents itself in the form: Before the creation of anything, nothingness existed. The somethingness of nothingness attains in the minds of some philosophers so convincing an aspect of reality, that they ascribe to it qualities and a mode of existence. Berdyaev finds in the nothingness that preceded creation the origin and abode of freedom, including the freedom of will.

> The world and the centre of the world—man—is the creation of God through Wisdom, through Divine Ideas, and at the same time it is the child of meonic uncreated freedom, the child of fathomless non-being. The element of freedom does not come from God the Father, for it is prior to being. . . . Fathomless freedom springing from non-being entered the created world, consenting to the act of creation.[6]

And he adds:

> If we think deeply and consistently we are compelled both to identify evil with non-being and to admit its positive significance. Evil is a return to non-being, a rejection of the world, and at the same time it has a positive significance because it calls forth as a reaction against itself the supreme creative power of the good.[7]

The phrase in all this that is perplexing is, I think, that which asserts that meonic freedom is "prior to be-

[6] Nicholas Berdyaev: *The Destiny of Man.*
[7] Ibid.

ing." If God is the ultimate and absolute Being, then the suggestion is—not merely that "nothing is prior to God" (which, in the purely negative sense, is an orthodox truism), but that this nothingness is a somethingness, with a property of its own, namely, Freedom, and a mode of existence of its own, namely, Time. For the words "prior to" suggest a priority *in Time*. The conclusion would seem to be that there was a time when God (who is Being) was not. Elsewhere, however, Berdyaev maintains that God exists in the mode of Eternity, which has no connection with Time at all.

Time is so intimately the mode of our own existence that it is equally difficult to conceive of Time apart from Being or of Being apart from Time. Perhaps this means that we ought not to try to conceive of them separately: for scientists frequently warn us that questions which produce meaningless answers usually turn out to have been meaningless questions. It may be more fruitful to consider Time as a part of creation, or perhaps that Time is necessarily associated with Being in Activity—that is, not with God the Father but with God the Son; with the Energy and not with the Idea.

This is where our analogy may be useful to us, by demonstrating the curious association of Not-Being with Being, and the still more curious effect that both exercise upon Time. What I want to suggest is that Being (simply *by* being) creates Not-Being, not merely contemporaneously in the world of Space, but also in the whole extent of Time behind it. So that though, in the absence of Being, it would be meaningless to say that Not-Being precedes Being; yet, in the presence of Being that proposition becomes both significant and true,

because Being has made it so. Or, to use the most familiar of all metaphors, "before" light, there was neither
light nor darkness; darkness is not darkness until light
has made the concept of darkness possible. Darkness
cannot say: "I precede the coming light," but there is
a sense in which light can say, "Darkness preceded
me."

Shakespeare writes *Hamlet*. That act of creation enriches the world with a new category of Being, namely:
Hamlet. But simultaneously it enriches the world with
a new category of Not-Being, namely: Not-Hamlet.
Everything other than *Hamlet*, to the farthest bounds
of the universe, acquires in addition to its former characteristics, the characteristic of being Not-Hamlet; the
whole of the past immediately and automatically becomes Not-Hamlet.

Now, in a sense, it is true to say that the past was
Not-Hamlet before *Hamlet* was created or thought-of;
it is true, but it is meaningless, since apart from *Hamlet*
there is no meaning that we can possibly attach to the
term Not-Hamlet. Doubtless there is an event, X, in
the future, by reference to which we may say that we
are at present in a category of Not-X, but until X
occurs, the category of Not-X is without reality. Only
X can give reality to Not-X; that is to say, Not-Being
depends for its reality upon Being. In this way we may
faintly see how the creation of Time may be said automatically to create a time when Time was not, and how
the Being of God can be said to create a Not-Being that
is not God. The bung-hole is as real as the barrel, but
its reality is contingent upon the reality of the barrel.

Arguing along these lines, we may make an attempt

to tackle the definition of Evil as the deprivation or the negation of the Good. If Evil belongs to the category of Not-Being, then two things follow. First: the reality of Evil is contingent upon the reality of Good; and secondly: the Good, by merely occurring, automatically and inevitably creates its corresponding Evil. In this sense, therefore, God, Creator of all things, creates Evil as well as Good, because the creation of a category of Good necessarily creates a category of Not-Good. From this point of view, those who say that God is "beyond Good and Evil" are perfectly right: He transcends both, because both are included within His Being. But the Evil has no reality except in relation to His Good; and this is what is meant by saying that Evil is negation or deprivation of Good.

But we have not quite finished with our Hamlet example. So long as Not-Being remains negative and inactive, it produces no particular effects, harmful or otherwise. But if Not-Hamlet becomes associated with consciousness and will, we get something which is not merely Not-Hamlet: we get Anti-Hamlet. Someone has become aware of his Not-Hamletness, and this awareness becomes a center of will and of activity. The creative will, free and active like God, is able to will Not-Being into Being, and thus produce an Evil which is no longer negative but positive.[8] This, according to the ancient myth of the Fall, is what happened to Men. They desired to be "as gods, knowing good and evil." God, according to St. Thomas Aquinas, knows Evil "by simple intelligence"—that is, in the category of

[8] Theologically: *privatio* issues in a real *depravatio*. (Robertson.)

Not-Being. But men, not being pure intelligences, but created within a space-time framework, could not "know" Evil as Not-Being—they could "know" it only by experience; that is, by associating their wills with it and so calling it into active Being. Thus the Fall has been described as the "fall into self-consciousness," and also as the "fall into self-will." And we may see why the Manichaeans were to some extent justified in connecting Evil with Matter; not that Matter in itself is Evil, but that it is the medium in which active Evil is experienced.

Once more, our literary analogy may be used to illustrate this distinction between Evil known by pure intelligence and Evil known by experience.

Our perfect writer is in the act of composing a work —let us call it the perfect poem. At a particular point in this creative act he selects the "right" word for a particular place in the poem. There is only the one word that is "dead right" in that place for the perfect expression of the Idea. The very act of choosing that one "right" word, automatically and necessarily makes every other word in the dictionary a "wrong" word. The "wrongness" is not inherent in the words themselves— each of them may be a "right" word in another place [9] —their "wrongness" is contingent upon the "rightness" of the chosen word. It is the poet who has created the "wrongness" in the act of creating the "rightness." In making a good which did not exist before he has simultaneously made an evil which did not exist before. Nor

[9] Always excepting, of course, words like "sportsdrome" and "normalcy," which are so steeped in sin that no place is "right" for them, except Hell, or a Dictionary of Barbarisms.

was there any way by which he could possibly make the Good without making the Evil as well.

Now, the mere fact that the choice of the "right" word *is* a choice implies that the writer is potentially aware of all the wrong words as well as the right one. In the creative act, his Energy (consciously or unconsciously) passed all the "wrong" possibilities in review as an accompaniment of selecting the right one. He may have seized immediately upon the right word as though by inspiration or he may actually have toyed with a number of the wrong ones before making the choice. It is immaterial which he did—the Energy has to give out more sweat and passion at some moments than at others. But potentially and contingently, his intelligence "knows" all the wrong words. He is free, if he chooses, to call all or any of those wrong words into active being within his poem—just as God is free, if He likes, to call Evil into active being. But the perfect poet does not do so, because his will is subdued to his Idea, and to associate it with the wrong word would be to run counter to the law of his being. He proceeds with his creation in a perfect unity of will and Idea, and behold! it is very good.

Unfortunately his creation is safe from the interference of other wills only as long as it remains in his head. By materializing his poem—that is, by writing it down and publishing it—he subjects it to the impact of alien wills. These alien wills can, if they like, become actively aware of all the possible wrong words and call them into positive being. They can, for example, misquote, misinterpret, or deliberately alter the poem. This evil is contingent upon the poet's original good: you cannot misquote a poem that is not there, and the poet is (in that sense) responsible for all subsequent misquotations of his work. But one can scarcely hold him guilty of them.

Misquotation, misinterpretation and deliberate distortion produce the same kind of evil in different ways. We may feel that they are quite dissimilar offenses. Misquotation arises from carelessness or bad memory; misinterpretation from lack of understanding; deliberate distortion from a perverted intention: we may call them mechanical (or material) defect, intellectual error, and moral wickedness. In fact, however, they have this much in common, that they all arise from the circumstance that the other person is not God and is trying to be "as God." The poet (within the terms of the analogy) is God—the one and only God of that particular creation. He is the only mind that knows its own Idea. If anybody else could be the god of the poem, his Idea would be identical with the poet's Idea, and his Energy would issue in the same "good" creation. But since that is not the case, the new will runs counter to "God's" Idea, and by associating itself with "wrong" words produces active Error.

To be sure, the new will may be full of excellent intentions. The better the intentions, the more strongly does the will associate itself with them, and the more disastrous the results. To say, carelessly, "caviare to the multitude" instead of "caviare to the general" is an error made almost without willfulness, which does comparatively little harm to *Hamlet*. It is more harmful to *Hamlet* to quote:

more honoured in the breach than in the observance

as though it meant "more often honoured" rather than "more properly honoured," because the Idea is more violently distorted, and the loss of Power is greater. But infinitely more damaging than either to the Power of *Hamlet* is to behave like David Garrick, and re-write *Hamlet* deliberately for the express purpose of improving it. This kind of grasping at equality with God really does do untold damage. It reduces a noble work of creation to nonsense; and the excuse that Garrick thought he was making it into a better play only aggravates the presumption.

The mind of man has always appreciated this ascending scale of Evil, from the material through the intellectual to the moral. It recognizes that the moral Evil is the worst, because it is associated with more will and more self-consciousness, and consequently with more Power. Power can proceed from Evil, as soon as Evil is called into active Being, because it then comes back as it were into touch with God, the ultimate Being and source of Power. For this reason it is said that all activity is of God—even evil activity. Such Power as anti-Hamlet possesses derives originally from the Power that is in *Hamlet,* without which it could have no Being.

What are we to do with the anti-Hamlets? In this particular case we can, to some extent, check the evil and prevent it from doing harm in the future, though its record of past evil remains. But there is a further thing we can do. We can redeem it. That is to say, it is possible to take its evil Power and turn it into active good. We can, for example, enjoy a good laugh at David Garrick. In so doing we, as it were, absorb the

Evil in the anti-Hamlet and transmute it into an entirely new form of Good. This is a creative act, and it is the only kind of act that will actually turn positive Evil into positive Good. Or, we can use the dreadful example of David Garrick for edification, which is what I have tried to do here, in the hope that this will prove to be a good, creative activity.

We can do this, only if we first get back into contact with the original great Idea that was in *Hamlet*—since we can never see how wrong Garrick was till we realize just how right Shakespeare was. In such ways, we can (while still thinking it a pity that David Garrick ever set pen to paper) enrich the world with more and more varied Goodness than would have been possible without the evil interference of David Garrick. What we must not do is to pretend that there never was a Garrick, or that his activities were not Evil. We must not, that is, try to behave as though the Fall had never occurred nor yet say that the Fall was a Good Thing in itself. But we may redeem the Fall by a creative act.

That, according to Christian doctrine, is the way that God behaved, and the only way in which we can behave if we want to be "as gods." The Fall had taken place and Evil had been called into active existence; the only way to transmute Evil into Good was to redeem it by creation. But, the Evil having been experienced, it could be redeemed only within the medium of experience—that is, by an incarnation in which experience was fully and freely in accordance with the Idea.

VIII

PENTECOST

*And if any man hear my words and believe not, I judge
him not; for I came not to judge the world, but to save the
world. He that rejecteth me, and receiveth not my words,
hath one that judgeth him: the word that I have spoken, the
same shall judge him in the last day.* —ST. JOHN xii. 47, 48

*If I go not away, the Comforter will not come unto you;
but if I depart, I will send him unto you.* —*Ibid.* xvi. 7

*Power
That through the growing faculties of sense
Doth like an agent of the one great Mind
Create, creator and receiver both.*
—WILLIAM WORDSWORTH: *The Prelude*

PENTECOST

WHEN the writer's Idea is revealed or incarnate by his Energy, then, and only then, can his Power work on the world. More briefly and obviously, a book has no influence till somebody can read it.

Before the Energy was revealed or incarnate it was, as we have seen, already present in Power within the creator's mind, but now that Power is released for communication to other men, and returns from their minds to his with a new response. It dwells in them and works upon them with creative energy, producing in them fresh manifestations of Power.

This is the Power of the Word, and it is dangerous. Every word—even every idle word—will be accounted for at the day of judgment, because the word itself has power to bring to judgment. It is of the nature of the word to reveal itself and to incarnate itself—to assume material form. Its judgment is therefore an intellectual, but also a material judgment. The habit, very prevalent today, of dismissing words as "just words" takes no account of their power. But once the Idea has entered into other minds, it will tend to reincarnate itself there with ever-increasing Energy and ever-increasing Power. It may for some time incarnate itself only in more words, more books, more speeches; but the day comes when it incarnates itself in actions, and this is its day of judgment. At the time when these words are being written, we are witnessing a fearful judgment of blood, resulting from the incarnation in deeds of an Idea to which, when it was content with a verbal revelation, we paid singularly little heed. Which Ideas are (morally) Good and which are anti-Good it is not the purpose of this book to discuss; what is now abundantly manifest is the Power. Any Idea whose Energy manifests itself in a Pentecost of Power is good from its own point of view. It shows itself to be a true act of creation, although, if it is an evil Idea, it will create to a large extent by active negation—that is to say, by destruction. The fact, however, that "all activity is of God" means that no creative Idea can be wholly destructive: some creation will be produced together with the destruction; and it is the work of the creative mind to see that the destruction is redeemed by its creative elements.

It is the business of education to wait upon Pentecost. Unhappily, there is something about educational syllabuses, and especially about examination papers, which seems to be rather out of harmony with Pentecostal manifestations. The Energy of Ideas does not seem to descend into the receptive mind with quite that rush of cloven fire which we ought to expect. Possibly there is something lacking in our Idea of education; possibly something inhibiting has happened to the Energy. But Pentecost will happen, whether within or without official education. From some quarter or other, the Power will descend, to flame or to smolder until it is ready to issue in a new revelation. We need not suppose that, because the mind of the reader is inert to Plato, it will therefore be inert to Nietzsche or Karl Marx. Failing those, it may respond to Wilhelmina Stitch or to Holly-wood. No incarnate Idea is altogether devoid of Power; if the Idea is feeble, the Energy dispersed, and the Power dim, the indwelling spirit will be dim, dispersed and feeble—but such as it is, so its response will be and such will be its manifestation in the world.

It is through the Power that we get a reflection in the mind of the world of the original Trinity in the mind of the writer. For the reader, that is, the book itself is presented as a threefold being.

First: the Book as Thought—the Idea of the book existing in the writer's mind. Of this, the reader can be aware only by faith. He knows that it does exist, but it is unknowable to him except in its manifestations. He can, of course, suppose if he likes that the book corresponds to nothing at all in the writer's mind; he can, if he likes, think that it got into its visible form by accident and that there is not and never was any such person as the writer. He is perfectly free to think these things, though in practice he seldom avails himself of this freedom. Where a book is concerned, the average man is a confirmed theist. There was, certainly, a little time ago, a faint tendency to polytheism among the learned. In particular cases, that is, where there was no exterior evidence about the writer, the theory was put forward that the *Iliad*, for example, and the *Song of Roland* were written by "the folk"; some extremists actually suggested that they "just happened"—though even such people were forced to allow the mediation of a little democracy of godlets to account for the material form in which these manifestations presented themselves. To-day, the polytheistic doctrine is rather at a discount; at any rate it is generally conceded that the Energy exhibited in written works must have emanated from some kind of Idea in a personal mind.

Secondly: the Book as Written—the Energy or Word incarnate, the express image of the Idea. This is the book that stands upon our shelves, and everything within and about it: characters, episodes, the succession of words and phrases, style, grammar, paper and ink, and, of course, the story itself. The incarnation of the Energy stands wholly within the space-time frame: it is written by a material pen and printed by a material machine upon material paper; the words were produced as a succession of events succeeding one another in time. Any timelessness, illimitability or uncreatedness which may characterize the book belongs not here but in the mind; the *body* of the Energy is a created thing, strictly limited by time and space, and subject to any accident that may befall matter. If we do not like it, we are at liberty to burn it in the market-place, or subject it to any other indignity, such as neglecting it, denying it, spitting upon it, or writing hostile reviews about it. We must, however, be careful to see that nobody reads it before we take steps to eliminate it; otherwise, it may disconcert us by rising again—either as a new Idea in somebody's mind, or even (if somebody has a good memory) in a resurrected body, substantially the same though made of new materials. In this respect, Herod showed himself much more competent and realistic than Pilate or Caiaphas. He grasped the principle that if you are to destroy the Word, you must do so before it has time to communicate itself. Crucifixion gets there too late.

Thirdly: the Book as Read—the Power of its effect upon and in the responsive mind. This is a very difficult thing to examine and analyze, because our own perception of the thing is precisely what we are trying to perceive. We can, as it were, note various detached aspects of it: what we cannot pin down and look at is the movement of our own mind. In the same way, we cannot follow the movement of our own eyes in a mirror. We can, by turning our head, observe them in this position and in that position with respect to our body, but never in the act of moving themselves from one position to the other, and never in the act of gazing at anything but the mirror. Thus our idea of ourself is bound to be falsified, since what to others appears the most lively and mobile part of ourself, appears to us unnaturally fixed. The eye is the instrument by which we see everything, and for that reason it is the one thing we cannot see with truth. The same thing is true of our Power of response to a book, or to anything else; incidentally, this is why books about the Holy Ghost are apt to be curiously difficult and unsatisfactory—we cannot really look at the movement of the Spirit, just because It is the Power by which we do the looking.

We may, however, note one or two things—fixed aspects of the Power. Like the Idea itself, it is immaterial and timeless. When we say we "know *Hamlet*," we do not mean merely that we can memorize the whole succession of words and events in *Hamlet*. We mean that we have in our minds an awareness of *Hamlet* as a complete whole—"the end in the beginning." We can prove this by observing how differently we feel when seeing a performance of *Hamlet* on the one hand and an entirely new play on the other. While watching the new play we are in contact with the Energy, which we experience as a sequence in time; we wonder "how it is going to work out." If, during the interval, we are asked what we think of it, we can give only a very incomplete answer. Everything depends, we feel, on the last act. But when the final curtain has come down, we feel quite differently towards the play—we can think of it as a whole, and see how all the episodes are related to one another to produce something inside our mind which is *more* than the sum-total of the emotions we experienced while sitting in the audience. It is in this timeless and complete form that it remains in our recollection: the Energy is now related to the Idea more or less as it was in the mind of the playwright: the Word has returned to the Father.

When we see *Hamlet* (or any other play that we already "know") we start already in this frame of mind. We are able, as the performance proceeds, to relate the part to the whole and the time-sequence to eternity at every point. Just as the writer realized while writing that there was a complete Idea in his mind, because, step by step, he found himself relating the progress of his work *to* that Idea, so also we realize while watching the play that there is a "whole *Hamlet*" in our own minds to which we are busily referring every word and action as it passes before us. Our knowledge of how the whole thing "hangs together" gives us a deeper understanding and a better judgment of each part, because we can now refer it, not only to the past but also to the future; and, more than that, to a unity of the work which exists for us right outside the sequence of time. It is as though the writer's Idea had passed from eternity into time and then back into eternity again—still the same Idea, but charged with a different emphasis of Power derived from our own response. Not only that: if it is a play like *Hamlet*, which has already stimulated powerful responses in the minds of other men, our personal response will be related to a greater unity which includes all those other foci of Power. Every scholar and critic who has written about *Hamlet*, every great actor who has ever played the part, every painter or musician who has found a source of power in *Hamlet*, retransmits that power to the spectator, in accordance with the capacity for response that is in each.

It is by this kind of process that words and phrases become charged with the Power acquired by passing through the minds of successive writers. Pure scientists (who find this particular kind of power embarrassing to them) are always struggling in vain to rid words of their power of association; and the ugly formations which they devise for this purpose have as their excuse their comparative freedom from the artist's brand of creative power. Here is a trifling example. I was once taken to task by an arms expert for using the word "dynamite" as a symbol of explosive force. He contended, very justly, that dynamite was out of date; we now knew a great many substances that exploded more readily and with more devastating effect. My defense was that the newer words, though associated with more material power, had fewer associations of literary power. "Dynamite" carries with it the accumulated power flowing from the Greek *dynamis*—such concepts, for example, as belong to the words dynamo, dynamic, dynasty, and so forth, and such literary associations as Hardy's *The Dynasts*. Hardy's poem brings with it the thought of Napoleon's explosion of power; "dynasty" taps the power of ancient Egypt as it is interpreted in our minds. The expression "tri-nitro-toluol" (which I might have chosen) is, at present at any rate, much less rich in verbal associative power; also, its actual syllables unfortunately associate themselves with such jingling compounds as "tol-de-rol" and "tooralooral"—formations which, however powerful in their own sphere, contribute little to the energetic expression of "explosive force."

It is interesting to rake into one's own mind and discover, if one can, what were the combined sources of power on which one, consciously or unconsciously, drew while endeavoring to express an idea in writing. Here, for instance, is a whole string of familiar passages which were obviously hovering about in my memory when I wrote a phrase in *The Nine Tailors*.

When the morning stars sang together, and all the sons of God shouted for joy.—*Book of Job*

Above it stood the seraphims: each one had six wings; with twain he covered his face, and with twain he covered his feet, and with twain he did fly.—*Book of the Prophet Isaiah*

He rode upon the cherubims and did fly; He came flying upon the wings of the wind.—*Psalms of David*

With Saintly shout and solemn Jubily,
Where the bright Seraphim in burning row
Their loud up-lifted Angel trumpets blow,

And the Cherubick host in thousand quires
Touch their immortal Harps of golden wires,
With those just Spirits that wear victorious Palms,
Hymns devout and holy Psalms
Singing everlastingly.

     Milton: *At a Solemn Musick*

 The carvèd angels, ever eager-eyed,
 Stand, where upon their heads the cornice rests,
With hair blown back, and wings put cross-wise on their
   breasts.   Keats: *The Eve of St. Agnes*

  Only they see not God, I know,
  Nor all that chivalry of His,
  The soldier-saints who, row on row,
  Burn upward each to his point of bliss.
    Browning: *The Statue and the Bust*

. . . incredibly aloof, flinging back the light in a dusky shimmer of bright hair and gilded outspread wings, soared the ranked angels, cherubim and seraphim, choir over choir, from corbel and hammer-beam floating, face to face up-lifted.—*The Nine Tailors*

In addition to the passages quoted, there is, of course, the direct association with actual angel-roofs, such as that in March Parish Church, which I know well, and pictures of others, such as that at Needham Market. Vaguely, too, I fancy, there was an echo of other, re-moter associations:

  . . . all the dim rich city, roof by roof,
  Tower after tower, spire beyond spire,
  By grove and garden-lawn and rushing brook,
  Climbs to the mighty hall that Merlin built.
  And four great zones of sculpture, set betwixt
  With many a mystic symbol, gird the hall:
  And in the lowest, beasts are slaying men,
  And in the second, men are slaying beasts,

And on the third are warriors, perfect men,
And on the fourth are men with growing wings,
And over all one statue in the mould
Of Arthur, made by Merlin, with a crown,
And peaked wings pointed to the Northern Star.
                    Tennyson: *The Holy Grail*

Four great figures the corners on,
Matthew and Mark and Luke and John.
        Camilla Doyle (a poem read years ago,
        the title of which I have quite for-
        gotten. This is itself "associated" with
        the children's rhyme about Matthew,
        Mark, Luke and John).

Where the walls
Of Magnus Martyr hold
Inexplicable splendour of Ionian white and gold.
                    T. S. Eliot: *The Waste Land*

A bracelet of bright hair about the bone.
                    John Donne: *The Funeral*

It is, of course, open to anyone to point out that these
great streams of power have been much diminished by
pouring through my narrow channel. That is quite true,
and is partly a measure of my lack of capacity and
partly a recognition of the fact that any passage within
a work demands a volume of power appropriate to its
place in the unity of that work and no more.[1] But what
is important, and not always understood in these days,
is that a reminiscent passage of this kind is *intended* to

[1] Readers who are interested in studying how a great writer may
incorporate and enhance the power of former writers, as well as of
his own previous achievements, should study M. R. Ridley's book:
Keats' Craftsmanship.

recall to the reader all the associated passages, and so put him in touch with the sources of power behind and beyond the writer. The demand for "originality"— with the implication that the reminiscence of other writers is a sin against originality and a defect in the work—is a recent one and would have seemed quite ludicrous to poets of the Augustan Age, or of Shakespeare's time. The traditional view is that each new work should be a fresh focus of power through which former streams of beauty, emotion, and reflection are directed. This view is adopted, and perhaps carried to excess, by writers like T. S. Eliot, some of whose poems are a close web of quotations and adaptations, chosen for their associative value; or like James Joyce, who makes great use of the associative value of sounds and syllables. The criterion is, not whether the associations are called up, but whether the spirits invoked by this kind of verbal incantation are charged with personal power by the magician who speeds them about their new business.

The Power—the Spirit—is thus a social power, working to bring all minds into its own unity, sometimes by similarity and at other times by contrast. There is a diversity of gifts, but the same spirit. Sometimes we feel that a critic or student of a man's work has "read into it" a good deal more than the first writer "meant." This is, perhaps, to have a rather confined apprehension of the unity and diversity of the Power. In the narrower sense, it is doubtless true that when Solomon or somebody wrote the *Song of Songs* he did not "mean" to write an epithalamium on the mystic nuptials of Christ with His Church. By the same process of reasoning, when Drayton wrote:

> Since there's no help, come, let us kiss and part;
> Nay, I have done: You get no more of me . . .

he did not *mean* to express the complicated emotion of impatience, relief, acceptance and forlorn hope which *you* experienced "at the last gasp of Love's latest breath." Nevertheless, he was a true prophet of your emotion, since he *did* express it, so that you feel the lines to have been written "for you." In coming into contact with his Power, through the ink-and-paper body of his Energy, you are taken up into the eternal unity of Drayton's Idea. You now lie within the orbit of the Power, which (immanent and transcendent) is also within you, and your response to it will bring forth further power, according to your own capacity and energy. If you react to it creatively, your response will again assume the form of: an Idea in your mind, the manifestation of that Idea in some form of Energy or Activity (speech, behavior or what not), and a communication of Power to the world about you.

This threefoldness in the reader's mind corresponds to the threefoldness of the work (Book-as-Thought, Book-as-Written, Book-as-Read), and that again to the original threefoldness in the mind of the writer (Idea, Energy, Power). It is bound to be so, because that is the structure of the creative mind. When, therefore, we consider Trinitarian doctrine about the universal Creator, this is what we are driving at. We are arguing on the analogy of something perfectly familiar to our experience. The implication is that we find the threefold structure in ourselves (who are the-Book-as-Read) because that is the actual structure of the universe (which is the-Book-as-Written), and that it is in the universe because it is in God's Idea about the universe (the-Book-as-Thought). Further, that this structure is in God's Idea because it is the structure of God's mind.

This is what the doctrine *means;* whether it is true or mistaken is another matter, but this is the Idea that is put forward for our response. There is nothing mythological about Christian Trinitarian doctrine: it is analogical. It offers itself freely for meditation and discussion; but it is desirable that we should avoid the bewildered frame of mind of the apocryphal Japanese gentleman who complained:

"Honourable Father, very good; Honourable Son, very good; but Honourable Bird I do not understand at all."

"Honourable Bird," however, has certain advantages as a pictorial symbol, since, besides reminding us of those realities which it does symbolize, it also reminds us that the whole picture is a symbol and no more. There have been people so literal-minded as to suppose that God the Father really *is* an old man with a beard, but remarkably few adult persons can ever have believed that the Holy Ghost really *was* a dove. In what we may call the "standard" pictorial symbol of the Holy Trinity, the emphasis is rather upon the diversity than upon the identity; it depicts the Unity-in-Trinity. The Father, usually conceived as an aged priest, robed and crowned, holds upon His knees the figure of Christ crucified; between them hovers the Dove. The pictures of the First and the Third Persons are pure intellectual

symbol—they represent nothing in time-space-matter;
but the picture of the Second Person is living symbol:
it represents an event in history. This is what our analogy would lead us to expect: it is only the Energy that
issues in a material Book-as-Written; the Idea and the
Power remain immaterial and timeless in their reflected
natures as the Book-as-Thought and the Book-as-Read.

A set of miniatures by Fouquet in the *Book of Hours
of Etienne Chevalier,* presents us, on the other hand,
with a very interesting pictorial symbol of the identity
of the diversity, the Trinity-in-Unity: here, Father,
Son and Holy Ghost are shown as all human, all young
and all exactly alike. This is the Trinity in the mind—
the essential identity of Idea, Energy and Power, which
is reflected as a Trinity in the work—the Book being
the same book, whether thought, written or read.

Of these two pictorial symbols, the former operates
to prevent the spectator from "confounding the Persons," and the latter, to prevent him from "dividing
the Substance."

"So that" (as the Athanasian Creed observes, in what
looks like a glimpse of the obvious, but is really as complex and profound as the obvious usually turns out to
be) "there is one Father, not three fathers, one Son, not
three sons, one Holy Ghost, not three holy ghosts. And
. . . the whole three Persons are consubstantial together, and co-equal."

IX

THE LOVE OF THE CREATURE

You asked for a loving God: you have one. The great spirit you so lightly invoked, the "lord of terrible aspect," is present: not a senile benevolence that drowsily wishes you to be happy in your own way, not the cold philanthropy of a conscientious magistrate, nor the care of a host who feels responsible for the comfort of his guests, but the consuming fire Himself, the Love that made the worlds, persistent as the artist's love for his work and despotic as a man's love for a dog, provident and venerable as a father's love for a child, jealous, inexorable, exacting as love between the sexes. —C. S. LEWIS: *The Problem of Pain*

There is some secret stirring in the world,
A thought that seeks impatiently its word.
—THOMAS LOVELL BEDDOES: (*Fragment*)

THE LOVE OF THE CREATURE

IT may be objected that the analogy we have been examining derives from the concept of the Platonic archetype, and is therefore unacceptable to those who reject Platonic ideal philosophy. That way of putting it is, however, not quite accurate; in fact, it puts the cart before the horse. To the creative artist (as we have seen) the archetype is not an *a priori* theory, but an experience.[1] From this experience he draws his analogy direct, and by its means illustrates and gives form to his philosophy, so that the philosophy is seen to derive from the analogy, and not vice versa. If at any points it coincides with Platonic or Christian philosophy, it does so as an independent witness. The experience is, of course, a particular experience—that of the human creator, and it is irrelevant for the analytical and uncreative critic to object to it on the ground that it is not *his* experience. For other minds, other analogies; but the artist's experience proves that the Trinitarian doctrine of Idea, Energy, Power is, quite literally, what it purports to be: a doctrine of the Creative Mind.

To the human maker, therefore, accustomed to look within himself for the extra-temporal archetype and pattern of his own creative work, it will also be natural to look beyond himself for the external archetype and

[1] See page 39. Actually, the concept is Augustinian rather than Platonic.

127

pattern of his own creative personality—the threefold Person in whose image he is made, as his own work is made in the image of himself.

At this point, however, he encounters certain difficulties which we shall have to consider, if we are not to be led away into undue literalism by our very natural anxiety to make our analogy go on all-fours.

The whole of existence is held to be the work of the Divine Creator—everything that there is, including not only the human maker and his human public, but all other entities "visible and invisible" that may exist outside this universe. Consequently, whereas the human writer obtains his response from other minds, outside and independent of his own, God's response comes only from His own creatures. This is as though a book were written to be read by the characters within it. And further: the universe is not a finished work. Every mind within it is in the position of the audience sitting in the theater and seeing the play for the first time. Or rather, every one of us is on the stage, performing a part in a play, of which we have not seen either the script or any synopsis of the ensuing acts.

This, it may be remarked, is no unusual situation, even among human actors. It is said of a famous actress [2] that for many years she played Lady Macbeth with great success, without having the faintest idea what the play was about or how it ended. She had never troubled to read it, and had always left the theater at the end of the sleep-walking scene without further inquiry as to the fate of the characters. Again, thousands of film

[2] I think it was Mrs. Pritchard, Johnson's "inspired idiot."

actors turn up daily at the studios, play through the shots in which they figure (sometimes in the right order, more often in the wrong order) and depart again, ignorant whether they are figuring in a tragedy, a comedy, or a melodrama; or what was the nature of the injury which caused them to shoot the stockbroker in the fifth reel or cut their own throats in the seventh. The actor on the stage of the universe cannot even go to the nearest cinema and see the result of his work when the sequences have been fitted together, for the film is still in the making. At the most, perhaps, towards the end of his life, he may see a few episodes in which he figured run through in the pages of contemporary history. And from the completed episodes of the past he may gather, if he is intelligent and attentive, some indication of the author's purpose.

There is one episode in particular to which Christianity draws his attention. The leading part in this was played, it is alleged, by the Author, who presents it as a brief epitome of the plan of the whole work. If we ask, "What *kind* of play is this that we are acting?" the answer put forward is: "Well, it is *this* kind of play." And examining the plot of it, we observe at once that if anybody in this play has his feelings spared, it is certainly not the Author.

This is perhaps what we should expect when we consider that a work of creation is a work of love, and that love is the most ruthless of all the passions, sparing neither itself, nor its object, nor the obstacles that stand in its way. The word "love" is by now so over-weighted with associations, from the most trifling to the most tremendous, that it is difficult to use it so as to convey a precise meaning to the reader; but here again the analogy we have chosen may be of some service.

Two popular interpretations of the word we can dismiss at once: the creator's love for his work is not a greedy possessiveness; he never desires to subdue his work to himself but always to subdue himself to his work. The more genuinely creative he is, the more he will want his work to develop in accordance with its own nature, and to stand independent of himself. Wellmeaning readers who try to identify the writer with his characters or to excavate the author's personality and opinions from his books are frequently astonished by the ferocious rudeness with which the author himself salutes these efforts at reabsorbing his work into himself. They are an assault upon the independence of his creatures, which he very properly resents. Painful misunderstandings of this kind may rive the foundations of social intercourse, and produce explosions which seem quite out of proportion to their apparent causes.

"I have ordered old brandy; I know you adore old brandy."

"What makes you think so?"

"Oh, I have read your books: I know Lord Peter is a great connoisseur of old brandy."

"He is; that needn't mean that I am."

"Oh! I thought you *must* be, as *he* is."

"What on earth have my tastes to do with his?"

It is quite possible that the author does like old brandy (though in this particular instance it happens not to agree with her). But what is intolerable is that the created being should be thus violently stripped of its own precious personality. The violence is none the less odious to the creator for the ingratiating smirk with which it is offered. Nor is the offense any more excusable when it takes the form of endowing the creature with qualities, however amiable, which run contrary to the law of its being:

"I am sure Lord Peter will end up as a convinced Christian."

"From what I know of him, nothing is more unlikely."

"But as a Christian yourself, you must *want* him to be one."

"He would be horribly embarrassed by any such suggestion."

"But he's *far* too intelligent and far too nice, not to be a Christian."

"My dear lady, Peter is not the Ideal Man; he is an eighteenth-century Whig gentleman, born a little out of his time, and doubtful whether any claim to possess a soul is not a rather vulgar piece of presumption."

"I am disappointed."

"I'm afraid I can't help that."

(*No; you shall not impose either your will or mine upon my creature. He is what he is, I will work no irrelevant miracles upon him, either for propaganda, or to curry favour, or to establish the consistency of my own principles. He exists in his own right and not to please you. Hands off.*)

Sometimes the suggestion to use force is accompanied by obliging offers of assistance. (Incidentally this type of petition must be extremely familiar to God Almighty.) Thus:

"Couldn't you make Lord Peter go to the Antarctic and investigate a murder on an exploring expedition?"

"Now, from what you know of him, can you imagine his

being inveigled into an Antarctic expedition, under any conceivable circumstances?"

"But it would be a new background—I could give you lots of authentic material."

"Thank you, you are very kind." (*Get to gehenna out of this and write up your own confounded material. Leave my creature alone—I will not "make" him do anything.*)

It will be seen that, although the writer's love is verily a jealous love, it is a jealousy *for* and not *of* his creatures. He will tolerate no interference either with them or between them and himself. But he does not desire that the creature's identity should be merged in his own, nor that his miraculous power should be invoked to wrest the creature from its proper nature.[3]

And if creative love is not possessive, neither is it sentimental. Writers have, admittedly, been sentimental over their creatures from time to time, but never without loss of creative power. The weakness that "interposed the glove of warning and the tear of sensibility between us and the proper ending of *Great Expectations*"[4] is a black crime against the creature. By not being permitted to suffer loss within their own microcosm, Pip and Estella have suffered irretrievable loss in the macrocosm. The sentimentality that distorted their true natures to give them an artificial happiness was no act of creative love. Bulwer-Lytton was the negating spirit that persuaded the god of their little universe to let the cup pass from them—the alteration would, he suggested, make the story "more acceptable." But criti-

---

[3] See Note "A" at end of chapter.
[4] G. K. Chesterton: *The Victorian Age in Literature.*

cal judgment has never accepted the falsification: the devil's gold turned to dust and dead leaves almost in the moment of purchase. It profits a book nothing to gain the whole circulating library, and lose its own soul.

When the story is by its nature a tragedy, then it is abundantly true that "each man kills the thing he loves," and that there are two ways of doing it. The cowardly writer, afraid to face the consequences for himself and his creation of the nature that he has created, "does it with a kiss"—by his kindness, that is, to his creatures, he will slobber away the whole situation, and so kill the work stone dead. "The brave man, with a sword," will execute judgment upon his creatures, and so slay *them* to preserve the life and power of the work. If, by this integrity, he incidentally alienates his readers and diminishes his immediate cash returns, his sacrifice is sure proof that he genuinely loves his creation.[5]

"Sacrifice" is another word liable to misunderstand-

---

[5] An unwise tenderness towards the created characters of fiction is, of course, only one of the forms which the writer's sentimentality may take. The tenderness may be poured out upon words or paragraphs of the book itself, so that the author becomes incapable of that firm massacre of unnecessary purple passages which is known to the literary trade as "murdering one's darlings." The waste-paper baskets of the world are stuffed with unpruned works whose creators suffered from this brand of sentimentality. (I have known a young woman who, in a similar spirit, could not bring herself to trim her "holiday snap-shots" so as to make them into well-balanced pictures. She protested that she "just couldn't bear" to sacrifice so much as a strip of blank sky or the out-of-focus intrusion of Uncle Bertie's boot from these creative efforts.) The tenderness which prompts the biographer to exhibit his subject as a dreary paragon of all the virtues is another, slightly more complicated, version of the sentimental treatment of an imagined hero.

ing. It is generally held to be noble and loving in proportion as its sacrificial nature is consciously felt by the person who is sacrificing himself. The direct contrary is the truth. To feel sacrifice consciously as self-sacrifice argues a failure in love. When a job is undertaken from necessity, or from a grim sense of disagreeable duty, the worker is self-consciously aware of the toils and pains he undergoes, and will say: "I have made such and such sacrifices for this." But when the job is a labor of love, the sacrifices will present themselves to the worker—strange as it may seem—in the guise of enjoyment.[e] Moralists, looking on at this, will always judge that the former kind of sacrifice is more admirable than the latter, because the moralist, whatever he may pretend, has far more respect for pride than for love. The Puritan assumption that all action disagreeable to the doer is *ipso facto* more meritorious than enjoyable action, is firmly rooted in this exaggerated valuation set on pride. I do not mean that there is no nobility in doing unpleasant things from a sense of duty, but only that there is more nobility in doing them gladly out of sheer love of the job. The Puritan thinks otherwise; he is inclined to say, "Of course, So-and-so works very hard and

[e] So Spenser:

> For some so goodly gratious are by kind,
> That every action doth them much commend,
> And in the eyes of men great liking find,
> Which others that have greater skill in mind,
> Though they enforce themselves, cannot attaine;
> *For everything to which one is enclin'd*
> *Doth best become and greatest grace doth gaine:*
> Yet praise likewise deserve good thewes enforst with paine.
>
> *Faery Queene*: VI. 11, 2

has given up a good deal for such-and-such a cause, but there's no merit in that—he enjoys it." The merit, of course, lies precisely in the enjoyment, and the nobility of So-and-so consists in the very fact that he is the kind of person to whom the doing of that piece of work is delightful.

It is because, behind the restrictions of the moral code, we instinctively recognize the greater validity of the law of nature, that we do always in our heart of hearts prefer the children of grace to the children of legality. We recognize a false ring in the demanding voice which proclaims: "I have sacrificed the best years of my life to my profession (my family, my country, or whatever it may be), and have a right to expect some return." The code compels us to admit the claim, but there is something in the expression of it that repels us. Conversely, however, the children of legality are shocked by the resolute refusal of the children of light to insist on this kind of claim and—still more disconcertingly—by their angry assertion of love's right to self-sacrifice. Those, for example, who obligingly inform creative artists of methods by which (with a little corrupting of their creative purpose) they could make more money, are often very excusably shocked by the fury with which they are sent about their business. Indeed, creative love has its darker aspects, and will sacrifice, not only itself, but others to its overmastering ends. Somerset Maugham, in *The Moon and Sixpence*, has given convincing expression to these dark fires of the artist's devouring passion; and the meaning of the story is lost unless we recognize that Strickland's terrible sacrifices, suffered and exacted, are the assertion of a love so tremendous that it has passed beyond even the desire of happiness. A passion of this temper does not resign itself to sacrifice, but embraces it, and sweeps the world up in the same embrace. It is not without reason that we feel a certain uneasy suspicion of that inert phrase, "Christian resignation"; an inner voice reminds us that the Christian God is Love, and that love and resignation can find no common ground to stand on. So much the human creator can tell us, if we like to listen to him. Our confusion on the subject is caused by a dissipation and eclecticism in our associations with the word "love." We connect it too exclusively with the sexual and material passions, whose anti-passion is possessiveness, and with indulgent affection, whose anti-passion is sentimentality. Concentrated, and freed from its anti-passions, love is the Energy of creation:

> In the juvescence of the year
> Came Christ the tiger—[7]

a disturbing thought.

> Tiger, tiger, burning bright
> In the forests of the night,
> What immortal hand or eye
> Could frame thy fearful symmetry? . . .
>
> And what shoulder and what art,
> Could twist the sinews of thy heart?
> And when thy heart began to beat,
> What dread hand? and what dread feet? . . .
>
> When the stars threw down their spears,
> And water'd heaven with their tears,

[7] T. S. Eliot: *Gerontion.*

Did he smile his work to see?
Did he who made the Lamb make thee? [8]

To that question, the creative artist returns an unqualified Yes, exciting thereby consternation, and the hasty passing of resolutions by the guardians of the moral code that artists are dangerous people and a subversive element in the state.

And the kings of the earth, and the great men and the rich men, and the chief captains, and the mighty men, and every bondman, and every free man, hid themselves in the dens and in the rocks of the mountains, and said to the mountains and rocks, Fall on us, and hide us from the face of him that sitteth on the throne, and from the wrath of the Lamb; for the great day of his wrath is come; and who shall be able to stand? [9]

Who indeed? Neither resistance nor resignation will do anything here. To Love-in-Energy, the only effective response is Love-in-Power, eagerly embracing its own sacrifice. In other words, the perfect work of love demands the co-operation of the creature, responding according to the law of its nature.

For the artist who handles inanimate matter, this co-operation is secured without the creature's self-consciousness or will, so long as the creator has rightly conceived the work in relation to the nature of his material. Inanimate matter, left to itself, tends to fall into randomness along the lines of least resistance, and this tendency determines its natural structure. It is the artist's business to see that this movement of the natural structure co-operates with the structure of his work.

[8] William Blake: *Songs of Experience.*
[9] Revelation of St. John vi. 16, 17.

The structure of sand does not, for example, adapt itself to the making of ropes, and the folly of the artist who attempts any such unco-operative scheme has passed into a proverb. Certain kinds of sand will, however, readily adapt themselves to the making of glass, though at the sacrifice of their original structure. With living, though unconscious, matter, the creator must still adapt the work to the material, though here he experiences something that can without undue anthropomorphism be called a "response"; plants "respond" to cultivation and cross-fertilization in a sense rather different from that in which iron may be said to "respond" to hammering. Animal matter, again, "responds" upon a rising scale of consciousness, until, with domesticated beasts, we approach very nearly to full self-conscious co-operation. In the relations of man with man, the co-operation contains the highest proportion of self-consciousness.

That no human maker can create a self-conscious being, we have already seen; and seen also that he is always urged by an inward hankering to do so, finding approximate satisfactions for this desire in procreation, in such relations as those of a playwright with his actors, and in the creation of imaginary characters. In all these relations, he is conscious of the same paradoxical need—namely, the complete independence of the creature, combined with its willing co-operation in his purpose in conformity with the law of its nature. In this insistent need he sees the image of the perfect relation of Creator and creature, and the perfect reconciliation of divine predestination with free created will.

In the creature also, he recognizes a division and a paradox. He is aware at once of its insistent urge to become manifest, and also, at the same time, a resistance to creation and a tendency to fall back into the randomness of negation. It is this resistance that Berdyaev calls the "dark meonic freedom"—the impulse to chaos. It is bound up with the natural law of matter, which is a law of increasing randomness as time goes on. From this point of view, there is some justification for connecting the evil and negative principle with the material part of the universe. But if matter and randomness are inextricably connected, so also are matter and life; we do not know life within the universe, except in association with matter, and the natural tendency of *living* matter is away from randomness and towards complexity and order. Sir James Jeans has pessimistically expressed the situation:

> If the inanimate universe moves in the direction we suppose, biological evolution moves like a sailor who runs up the rigging in a sinking ship.[10]

The struggle between order and chaos is thus not peculiar to the nature of man; it is found in all life, and perhaps even in all matter, since matter (whether or not it is capable of actually producing life) certainly provides the only known medium for the manifestation of life. This clash and paradox lies at the base of the Doctrine of the Fall, which by some ancient writers was held to be a fall of the whole material universe, though by others, the fall is held to consist in man's ranging of his self-conscious will on the side of the chaotic as against the orderly, of destruction as against

[10] Sir James Jeans: *Eos.*

life. Inside the time-scheme, there appears to be no possible solution for the antinomy; the synthesis belongs to an eternity which is outside time altogether. This, our analogy would lead us to expect, since all the difficulties and oppositions of a work of creation belong precisely to the effort to make it manifest in material form and in the time-sequence.

The resistance to creation which the writer encounters in his creature is sufficiently evident, both to himself and to others—particularly to those others who have the misfortune to live with him during the period when his Energy is engaged on a job of work. The human maker is, indeed, almost excessively vocal about the perplexities and agonies of creation and the intractability of his material. Almost equally evident, however, though perhaps less readily explained or described, is the creature's violent urge to be created. To the outsider, the spectacle of a writer "taken ill with an idea" usually presents itself as a subject for unseemly mirth. The "Spring poet" is the perennial butt of the plain man, just as, on the stage, any reference to child-birth is a signal for hoots of merriment, especially from the male members of the audience. In both cases, the ridicule is largely defensive—the nervous protest of the negative and chaotic against the mysterious and terrible energy of the creative. But that a work of creation struggles and insistently demands to be brought into being is a fact that no genuine artist would think of denying. Often, the demand may impose itself in defiance of the author's considered interests and at the most inconvenient moments. Publisher, bank-balance, and even the conscious intellect may argue that the writer should

pursue some fruitful and established undertaking; but
they will argue in vain against the passionate vitality
of a work that insists on manifestation. The strength of
the insistence will vary from something that looks like
direct inspiration to something that resembles a mere
whim of the wandering mind; but whenever the creature's desire for existence is dominant, everything else
will have to give way to it; the writer will push all other
calls aside and get down to his task in a spirit of mingled
delight and exasperation. Because of this, the artist
ought, above all men, to be chary of basing his philosophy of life on the assumption that "we are brought
into this world by no choice of our own." That may
be so, but he has no means of proving it, and the analogy
of his own creative experience offers evidence to the
contrary. He knows very well that he, in his work, is
for ever ground between the upper and nether mill-
stones of the universal paradox. His creature simultaneously demands manifestation in space-time and stub-
bornly opposes it; the will of his universe is to life as
implacably as it is to chaos.[11]

But there is this difference: that for the satisfaction
of its will to life it depends utterly upon the sustained
and perpetually renewed will to creation of its maker.
The work can live and grow on the sole condition of
the maker's untiring energy; to satisfy its will to die,
he has only to stop working. In him it lives and moves
and has its being, and it may say to him with literal

---

[11] It is, of course, irrelevant to object that this "creature" struggling towards manifestation is "really" only a part of the maker's
own ego. *All* creatures are a part of the Maker's mind, and have no
independent existence till they attain partial independence by manifestation.

truth, "Thou art my life, if thou withdraw, I die." If the unselfconscious creature could be moved to worship, its thanks and praise would be due, not so much for any incidents of its structure, but primarily for its being and its identity. It would not, if it were wise, petition its maker to wrest its own nature out of truth on any pretext at all, since (as we have seen) any violence of this kind serves only to diminish its vitality and destroy its identity. Still less would it desire him to subdue his own will or alter his purpose in the writing, since any such deviation from the Idea will disintegrate the work and send the fragments sliding the random way to chaos. If it possessed will and consciousness, it could achieve life and individual integrity only by co-operating with the Energy to interpret the Idea in Power.

The human maker, working in unselfconscious matter, receives no worship from his creatures, since their will is no part of his material; he can receive only the response of their nature, and he is alone in fault if that response is not forthcoming. If he tortures his material, if the stone looks unhappy when he has wrought it into a pattern alien to its own nature, if his writing is an abuse of language, his music a succession of unmeaning intervals, the helpless discomfort of his material universe is a reproach to him alone. Similarly, if he respects and interprets the integrity of his material, the seemliness of the ordered work proclaims his praise, and his only, without will, but in a passive beauty of right structure. If he works with plants, with animals or with men, the co-operative will of the material takes part in the work in an ascending scale of conscious response and personal readiness to do him honor. But a perfect identity of conscious will between himself and the creature can never be attained; identity is in fact attained in inverse ratio to the consciousness of the creature. A perfect identity of the creature with its creator's will is possible only when the creature is unselfconscious: that is, when it is an externalization of something that is wholly controlled by the maker's mind. But even this limited perfection is not attainable by the human artist, since he is himself a part of his own material. So far as his particular piece of work is concerned, he is Godlike—immanent and transcendent; but his work and he both form part of the universe, and he cannot transcend the universe. All his efforts and desires reach out to that ideal creative archetype in whose unapproachable image he feels himself to be made, which can make a universe filled with free, conscious and co-operative wills; a part of his own personality and yet existing independently within the mind of the maker.

NOTE "A"—*Independence of the Creature*

It is here that we reach the great watershed that divides Imagination from Fantasy—activities often confused by psychologists. "The subject," they say, "invents things about himself"; as though there were but one kind of invention. In fact, the two things have almost nothing in common, except that the personality is the raw material of both. They can exist side by side in the same man, or the same child, and are distinguished by him immediately and infallibly.

Fantasy works inwards upon its author, blurring the boundary between the visioned and the actual, and associating itself ever more closely with the Ego, so that the child who has fantasied himself a murderer ends by becoming a

Loeb or a Leopold. The creative Imagination works out-
wards, steadily increasing the gap between the visioned and
the actual, till this becomes the great gulf fixed between art
and nature. Few writers of crime-stories become murderers
—if any do, it is not as a result of identifying themselves
with their murderous heroes. Detective novelists do not
even fancy themselves much as investigators in real life,
though newspaper editors delude themselves that they do,
and make the author's life a burden by urging him to pro-
pound his own solution of the latest Trunk Murder or un-
dertake wearisome railway journeys to report the current
Torso Mystery on the spot.

It is hard to persuade psychologists that this distinction
between Imagination and Fantasy is fundamental—chiefly
because of their rooted refusal to receive the writer's testi-
mony in his own behalf. It is as though they insisted on as-
suring a gourmet that there was no real difference between
assafoetida and Lafitte, and that any distinction made by his
palate was a mere rationalization of some accidental collision
with assafoetida in his infancy. It is, of course, undeniable
that, when analysis is carried to the final stage, assafoetida
and Lafitte, together with the moon and green cheese, can
be resolved into the same atomic components, only rather
differently arranged. The same thing may be said of Imagination and Fantasy: the personality is the raw material of
both; the only difference is in what becomes of it. The
stronger the creative impulse, the more powerful is the urge
away from any identification of the Ego with the created
character.

Creative Imagination is thus the foe and antidote to fantasy—a truth recognized by psychologists in practice, but
frequently obscured in their writings by a muddled use of
the two terms as though they were interchangeable. Evidence of a habit of fantasy in a child is no proof of creative
impulse: on the contrary. The child who relates his fantasied adventures *as though they were fact* is about as far
removed from creativeness as he can possibly be; these

dreamy little liars grow up (if into nothing worse) into the feeble little half-baked poets who are the irritation and despair of the true makers. The child who is creative tells himself stories, as they do, but objectively. They usually center about some hero of tale or history, and are *never* confused in his mind with the ordinary day-dreams in which he sees himself riding rough-shod over the grown-ups or rescuing beloved prefects from burning buildings. Even if he does dramatize himself, and make "the bard the hero of the story," this is *pure* dramatization, and can be carried on parallel with his consciousness of real life, without ever at any point meeting it. It is not that the one kind of fancy develops into the other; they are completely and consciously independent. Accordingly, the first literary efforts of the genuinely creative commonly deal, in a highly imitative manner, with subjects of which the infant author knows absolutely nothing, such as piracy, submarines, snake-infested swamps, or the love-affairs of romantic noblemen. The well-meant exhortations of parents and teachers to "write about something you really know about" should be (and will be) firmly ignored by the young creator as yet another instance of the hopeless stupidity of the adult mind. Later in life, and with increased practice in creation, the drive outward becomes so strong that the writer's whole personal experience can be seen by him objectively as the material for his work.

I am not arguing with the authorities about this; I am telling them, because it is a thing that they often find very puzzling. The child who dresses up as Napoleon, and goes about demanding the respect due to Napoleon, is not necessarily a little paranoiac with a Napoleon-fixation; he is just as likely to be an actor.

X

SCALENE TRINITIES

God made man in His own image.
—The Book of Genesis

What a piece of work is a man! . . . in apprehension how like a god! —WILLIAM SHAKESPEARE: *Hamlet*

I have thought some of nature's journeymen had made men and not made them well, they imitated humanity so abominably. *—Ibid.*

Except a man believe rightly, he cannot be saved.
—Athanasian Creed

SCALENE TRINITIES

THE father-similitude of Godhead points to the perfect human parent; though this phenomenon is as rare as that normal eyesight by which, as a never-witnessed yet faithfully worshiped ideal, the oculist measures all the actual vision he has to deal with. So the Creator-similitude points to the perfect human artist. There are, however, no perfect artists—a fact on which literary criticism (an art-form with an exceptionally strong bias to death and destruction) tends to lay an almost exaggerated emphasis. The imperfections of the artist may be conveniently classified as imperfections in his trinity—a trinity which, like that Other to which it serves as analogy, must, if the work is to be saved, be thought of as having all its persons consubstantial and co-equal. The co-equality of the Divine Trinity is represented in pictures and in Masonic emblems as an equilateral triangle; but the trinity of the writer is seldom anything but scalene, and is sometimes of quite fantastic irregularity.

At the end of Chapter VIII, I quoted a verse of the Athanasian Creed. In my childhood, I remember feeling that this verse formed a serious blot upon a fascinating and majestic mystery. It was, I felt, quite unnecessary to warn anybody that there was "one Father, not three fathers; one Son, not three sons; one Holy Ghost, not three holy ghosts." The suggestion seemed quite foolish. It was difficult enough to imagine a God who was Three and yet One; did anybody exist so demented as to conceive of a ninefold deity? Three fathers was a plurality excessive even to absurdity. I found myself blushing faintly at the recitation of words so wildly unrelated to anything that the queerest heathen in his blindness was likely to fancy for himself. But critical experience has persuaded me that the Fathers of the Western Church knew more about human nature than I did. So far as the analogy of the human creator goes, their warning is justified. Writer after writer comes to grief through the delusion that what Chesterfield calls a "whiffling Activity" will do the work of the Idea; that the Power of the Idea in his own mind will compensate for a disorderly Energy in manifestation; or that an Idea is a book in its own right, even when expressed without Energy and experienced without Power. Many an unreadable monument of scholarship is exposed as the creature of three fathers; many a column of sob-stuff betrays the uncontrolled sensibility of three impression-able ghosts; many a whirlwind bustle of incoherent epi-sode indicates the presence of three sons at the head of affairs. None of the works thus produced need be a bad book in the sense of being written with willful careless-ness or in open contempt of artistic truth: "there are many ways in which poetry can go wrong, and an im-purity in the intention is only one of them." [1] Their writers are not artistic atheists, but only heretics, cling-ing with invincible ignorance to a unitarian doctrine of creation. And it is true that even in them a complete trinity must be to some extent engaged upon the work,

[1] C. S. Lewis: *The Allegory of Love.*

otherwise they could not write at all. But their work is hampered by their lop-sided doctrine, and they create wrongly because they do not "rightly believe." We may properly and profitably amuse ourselves by distinguishing those writers who are respectively "father-ridden," "son-ridden," and "ghost-ridden." It is the mark of the father-ridden that they endeavor to impose the Idea directly upon the mind and senses, believing that this is the whole of the work. In their very different ways, the dry-as-dust scholar is a type of these, and so is Blake wrestling with the huge cloudy cosmogonies and highly-personal symbolisms of the Prophetic Books. It is as though they were trying to get their message through without the full mediation of the son; while their ghost only mutters to their own souls in the secret places of the innermost, and is never poured out in power on the earth. Father-ridden also is that very familiar and faintly comic figure of the man who "has the most marvellous idea for a book, if only he had time to sit down and write it." [2] He genuinely believes that to the operations of the Energy time and a chair are the sole necessities, and that the son, like the father, is without sweat or passion.

Among the son-ridden, we may place such writers as Swinburne, in whom the immense ingenuity and sensuous loveliness of the manner is developed out of all

[2] When the artist has the book complete in his head before writing it down (see p. 41) the son is, of course, present in full activity with much of the work (e.g., style, characterization, sequence of episodes) already consciously realized; but this is not the case with the ingenuous gentleman in question, as we soon discover if we ask him to explain his idea. What is lacking in him is not time or a chair, but the first notion of how to set about the job.

proportion to the tenuity of the ruling idea. Their ghosts enjoy a kind of false Pentecost, thrilling and moving the senses but producing no genuine rebirth of the spirit. Of these, too, are the Euphuists and the empty wits; the prestidigitators of verbal arabesque and rime leonine; the alembicated, the pretentious and the precious, and those who (like Meredith at his worst) wrap up the commonplace in tortuous complexities—all those, in fact, whose manner has degenerated into mannerism. So also are the poets who startle the eye with nice derangements of capital letters and epithets staggered about the page. Here, I think, we must class the portmanteau-wordage of James Joyce, in which the use of verbal and syllabic association is carried so far that its power of unconscious persuasion is lost and the reader's response is diverted by a conscious ecstasy of enigma-hunting, like a pig rooting for truffles.

Anna Livia Plurabelle is at once womankind and the river Liffey (*amnis Livia* in Latin) and the beauty made of many beauties, as the river is the confluence of many streams. As the two washerwomen—themselves semi-mythological figures—recount her story to their paddling of the dirty clothes on the stones, they bring the names of hundreds of rivers into their talk. One of them cannot hear well, for the cotton in her ears: "It's that irrawaddy I've stoke in my aars. It all but husheth the lethest sound," she says. This is not mere rendering into a lisping brogue of the words: "It's this here wadding I've stuck in my ears. It all but hushes the least sound": it is the evocation of Lethe, the stream that flows through Hades, of the Aar river in Switzerland, of the Stoke, in England, and of an Indo-Chinese river, the Irawaddy.[3]

[3] Babette Deutsch: *This Modern Poetry.*

How clever, we admit; how ingenious and entertaining! Educative, too, like the more instructional kind of cross-word, if one were to go conscientiously through the "hundreds of rivers" with a gazetteer and an atlas. It would make a good "quiz" competition for the schoolroom. But what will become of the mood which the evocation of Lethe should engender?

The apologist continues: "Some of Joyce's neologisms need no elucidation. . . . A word like thonthorstrok carries more literary suggestions, combining as it does the idea of thunderbolt, stroke of lightning and Thor, the Hammerer, the Norse God of thunder." Well, so it does: but no more than the word "thunderstroke" carries in itself, and in fact considerably less, since the neologism limits the associations to those to which its eccentricity draws conscious attention, whereas "thunderstroke" calls up to the subliminal memory not only the associations "thunder," "lightning," and "Thor," but also *every* verbal and visual image accrued to it through many centuries, from Jupiter Tonans to the cannon in the Valley of Death, from Job and the Psalms to the two Boanerges and the apocalyptic thunderings that proceeded out of the Throne. In the intellectual pastime of dissecting-out "thonthorstrok" we become actively alert and thus impervious to subconscious suggestion; so that in our astonishment we are scarcely even receptive to our own kinship with Robinson Crusoe, who, beholding a like unprecedented phenomenon, "stood like one thunder-struck, or as if I had seen an apparition." In thus attempting to do by mechanical contrivance the work that should be done by "the response in the lively soul," the son usurps the domain of the spirit, and the father is smothered and lost in the dusty struggle.

The ghost-ridden writer, on the other hand, conceives that the emotion which he feels is in itself sufficient to awaken response, without undergoing discipline of a thorough incarnation, and without the coherence that derives from reference to a controlling idea. Such a man may write with the tears streaming down his cheeks, and yet produce nothing but turgid rhetoric, flat insipidity, or the absurdities of an Amanda Ros. The actor who passionately feels every line he speaks, so that sobs choke his utterance and agitation paralyzes his limbs will, if he relies solely upon this personal responsiveness, succeed only in choking and paralyzing the response of his audience. There is perpetual argument on this point: whether or not the actor should "live" his part; whether it is necessary to feel in order (as the common phrase goes) "to play with feeling." It is true that an implicit reliance on technique (which is the besetting heresy of the son-ridden) will reduce the art of acting to an assemblage of mechanical tricks, but, says Coquelin, "if I refuse to believe in art without nature I will not in the theatre have nature without art." And he tells the following tale about Edwin Booth, who, let us remember, was no incompetent, but one of the leading tragedians of his period:

One night he was playing *Le Roi S'Amuse*. The part was one of his best, and he enjoyed playing it. This time he satisfied himself even better than usual; the force of the situations, the pathos of the language worked on him so powerfully that he identified himself completely with his character. Real tears fell from his eyes, his voice was broken with

emotion; real sobs choked him, and it seemed to him that
he had never played so well. The performance over, he saw
his daughter hurrying towards him; she, his truest critic,
had been watching the scene from a box and was hastening
anxiously to inquire what was the matter, and how it happened that he had played so badly that night.[4]

Coquelin's conclusion is "that in order to call forth
emotion we ourselves must not feel it"; he does not say
that we must never have felt it, but only that, "the
actor must in all circumstances remain the absolute
master of himself." What he is trying to tell us is that
the artist must not attempt to force response by direct
contact with any response of his own; for spirit cannot
speak to spirit without intermediary. To interpret sensibility to sensibility we must have, not only the controlled technique of the Energy ordering the material
expression, but also the controlling Idea, "without parts
or passions" that, moving all things, "doth itself un-
moved abide." There must, in all art, be this hard core
or containing sphere (whichever metaphor is preferred)
of the unimpassioned. Otherwise the response of the
ghost to the son is uncritical, lacking any standard of
self-measurement.

It is, of course, only from time to time that the work
of good writers becomes "ridden" by one or other person of their trinity; though this does occasionally happen even to the best of them, when it causes them to
produce what look like unkind parodies of their own
style. But all writers (being human, however good)
tend to have their trinities permanently a little out of
true—slightly scalene—so that they may be divided into

[4] Constant Coquelin: *L'Art du Comédien.*

the father-centered, the son-centered and the ghost-centered. Thus, Blake at his most lucid, tender and lyrical, still displays the close-knit intellectual coherence and the serene detachment of the fatherhood: his fiercest passions have something cosmic and impersonal about them. It is probably this quality that provokes Lytton Strachey to charge him with being "inhuman." [5] Much of the somewhat meaningless controversy between the Classicists and the Romanticists is at bottom a temperamental incompatibility between the father-centered and the ghost-centered. And, on the other hand, many writers whose work is in general lop-sided and unsatisfactory will every so often achieve a stray poem or isolated phrase in which everything that was dim and scattered seems to come suddenly into focus, and which stands out from all their other performance with a unique brilliance and "rightness," like the image in a stereoscope at the moment of perfect superimposition. These, I fancy, are the moments when the writer's trinity has temporarily adjusted itself—when, for once, Idea, Energy and Power are consubstantial and coequal. The effect, when it does occur, is so dramatic that we may find it hard to believe that we are still dealing with the same writer. Critics of Elizabethan Drama, in fact, seldom even try to believe it, but promptly attribute the dazzling intruder to the interpolating hand of

[5] It ought not to be, but probably is, necessary to make plain at this point that it is not loftiness of theme and language that is the distinguishing characteristic of the father-centered, but the fact that all the writer's work and every part of it can be referred to a coherent and controlling unity of Idea. Blake, Aquinas, Euclid, and Bach are all patricentric, and so is Lewis Carroll in the "Alice" books; but Milton is not, nor Donne, though the father is powerful in both of them.

Shakespeare. Yet the phenomenon undoubtedly occurs, the best-known instance being, I suppose, the famous line:

A rose-red city half as old as time [6]—

ten syllables which have sufficed to render their creator immortal, though nowhere else in the poem, nor (so far as I know) in the rest of his creation, did the worthy gentleman present to the world a single memorable phrase.

To be father-centered, son-centered, or ghost-centered is not a major heresy or a mortal sin; in the general imperfection of human nature it is at most to be classed as the venial and unavoidable effect of original sinfulness. The image of God is a little out of drawing: if it were not, we should not merely become "as gods"— we should *be* gods. What is really damaging to a writer's creation is a serious and settled weakness in any side of his Trinity. Thus, a confirmed feebleness in the "father," or Idea, betrays itself in diffusion, in incoherence, in the breach of the Aristotelian unity of action or, still more disastrously, of the over-riding unity of theme. Not all works of rambling and episodic *form* are "fatherless" creations; form is the domain of the son, and a rambling form, like that of the picaresque novel, may be exquisitely and rightly adapted to the exact expression of the Idea. But if there is no unity of Idea within which the whole meandering structure can be included; or if the work, having started out as one kind of thing, ends up as another kind of thing; or if it contradicts its own nature and purpose in the process of development; or if (and this happens curiously often)

[6] Dean Burgon: *Petra: Newdigate Prize Poem*, 1845.

it enchants us in the reading by the elegant succession of its parts, and yet leaves in our memories no distinct impression of itself as a whole—in such cases, there is something radically wrong with its paternal Idea. There are, of course, writers who pride themselves on never planning out a book beforehand. If they are telling the truth, they are heretics—but very often they make these claims with their tongues in their cheeks. It is easy enough to test their statements. When their creation is successful as a work of art, the end-product will always disclose a unity of tone and theme which quite certainly did not come there by accident. *Tristram Shandy*, for example, the most willful of all these pretenders to incoherence, is held together by a bland uniformity of style and a methodical lack of method that bear witness to the cunning co-operation of father and son in its creation. For genuine incoherence and atrophy of the fatherhood, we must go to such an example as the huge, helpless collection of disconnected beauties that make up the scattered corpus of Beddoes' Dramas. Here, everything is lovely, everything is powerful in fragments; but the power and beauty of the work *as a whole* scarcely exist. It is a scrap-heap of discarded beginnings, canceled endings, episodes without connection, connecting passages that link nothing, actions without motive, scenes that lead up to situations which never occur, speeches that contradict the character of the speakers, characters whose aspect is only a looming bulk of form without feature. There is no unity, unless a general morbid preoccupation with death can be held to constitute unity; there is no real direction of the Energy, and no wholeness of conception. Kelsall's description of Beddoes' creative behavior shows clearly enough where the weakness lies:

His poetic composition was then [*in his youth*] exceedingly facile: More than once or twice has he taken home with him at night some unfinished act of a drama, in which the editor [*Kelsall himself*] had found much to admire, and, at the next meeting, has produced a new one, similar in design, but filled with other thoughts and fancies, which his teeming imagination had projected, in its sheer abundance, and not from any feeling, right or fastidious, of unworthiness in its predecessor. Of several of these very striking fragments, large and grand in their aspect as they each started into form,

Like the red outline of beginning Adam,

. . . the only trace remaining is literally the impression thus deeply cut into their one observer's mind.

This is the picture of a brilliant Energy, accompanied by an impressive Power, but disintegrated by lack of reference to a strong Idea. In later life, the easy fluidity that could thus carelessly create and destroy becomes a restless dissatisfaction; the writer refers irritably to his own work: "My cursed fellows in the jest-book [the unfinished drama, *Death's Jest-book*] would palaver immeasurably, and I could not prevent them"; "I often very shrewdly suspect that I have no real poetical call"; "I have no business to expect any great distinction as a writer . . . read only an act of Shakespear . . . or in fact anything deeply, naturally, sociably felt, and then take to these Jest-books—you will feel at once how forced, artificial, insipid, etc, etc, all such things are"; "the never-ending Death's Jest-book . . . the ill-fated play" . . . "a volume of prosaic poetry and poetical prose. It will contain half a dozen tales, comic, tragic and dithyrambic, satirical and semi-moral; perhaps half a hundred lyrical Jews-harpings in various styles and humours, and the still-born D.J.B."; "the endless D.J.B."; "the unhappy Jest-book." And finally, after his second attempt at suicide: "I ought to have been among other things a good poet; life was too great a bore . . ."[7] None of his dramas was, in fact, ever finished, except the early work, *The Brides' Tragedy*, nor was the contemplated volume of poetry and prose ever published; his whole creative history is that of great rivers running into the sand: "Dissatisfaction," he wrote, "is the lot of the poet, if it be that of any being; and therefore the gushings of the spirit, these pourings out of their innermost on imaginary topics, because there was no altar in their home worthy of the libation." It is certain that no poet whose trinity was strongly "fathered" could have written that last sentence; yet in everything but that absence of Idea, purpose, integrating wholeness, Beddoes had the quality of a great poet.

It is noticeable, by the way, that Beddoes was always eager for criticism and expressed himself surprisingly ready to alter his work to conform with other people's opinion. "Am I right in supposing that you would denounce, and order to be re-written, all the prose scenes and passages?—almost all the 1st and 2nd, great part of the 3rd act, much of the two principal scenes of the 4th, and the 5th to be strengthened and its opportunities better worked on? But you see this is no trifle, though I

[7] Letters: *Passim.*

believe it ought to be done." [8] "You will probably by this time have heard from Proctor and Bourne the decision of the higher powers . . . the play is to be revised and improved. . . . I have requested Proctor . . . to specify his objections, and as soon as he has done that, I shall do the same by you—What you have brought forward is, I believe, quite right and shall be adopted. . . . Proctor has denounced the carrion crows: [9]—I can spare them: but he has also as 'absolutely objectionable' anathematised Squats on a Toadstool,[9] with its crocodile—which I regard as almost necessary to the vitality of the piece. What say you? If a majority decide against it, I am probably wrong." [10] And so forth. It is true that the majority of these drastic reconstructions were never carried out; but what writer whose trinity was strongly co-ordinated would even dream of revising his work to conform with the majority report of a committee? Those whose Idea is in full control are especially obstinate and impervious to criticism; for in speaking for the father they speak with authority and not as the scribblers. One has only to compare the indifference and indecision of Beddoes with the independence of Blake, engraving his own verses in a stubborn isolation and damning the well-meant suggestions of his friends, to realize the gulf that yawns between the unfathered and the father-centered artist.

Blake and Beddoes present themselves very conveniently for the comparison of strength and weakness in the fatherhood. They were almost contemporaries

[8] Letter to Proctor, 19.4.29.
[9] Song in *Death's Jest-book*.
[10] Letter to Kelsall, 30.4.29.

(their lives overlapping by twenty years); they were equally isolated from the spirit of their age; and they were both poets of lofty and puissant quality. It is very much more difficult to find memorable examples of comparative strength and weakness in the sonhood. Everything in the visible structure of the work belongs to the son; so that a really disastrous failure in this person of the trinity produces not a good writer with a weakness, but simply a bad writer. There are too many of these for easy selection; moreover, the judgment upon bad writing is oblivion, so that the dreadful example, when found, is not likely to be familiar. We are, however, sufficiently familiar with those in whom the son is, to all intents and purposes, lacking altogether. They are the "mute, inglorious Miltons," of whom we, in our uncritical way, are rather apt to imagine that (like the monkey) they could say a great deal if they only chose, or if some accident of circumstance did not prevent them. That is a complete misunderstanding. They could not ever speak, for the thing wanting in them is precisely the activity of speech. Indeed, the phrase "mute *Miltons*" is either misleading or else apt by sheer force of self-contradiction; Milton being, as it happens, a poet in whom the son is particularly strong. What is actually meant is that these unfortunate people are, in their way, capable of entertaining an Idea and of feeling its responsive Power, but that they cannot give expression to it in creation, because they are empty of that Energy "by whom all things are made." The adjective "inglorious" is right—even more comprehensively right than we usually realize. It is not merely that they receive no glory of men; it is that they cannot themselves glorify the Idea or evoke its Power in glory within the universe; for the father can be glorified *only* in the son.

Thus, taking the mute Miltons as our starting-point, we can go on to observe that the distinguishing mark of the sonless is to be frustrate and inexpressive. They are those unhappiest of living men, the uncreative artists. The common man, who knows and dreads them, has his own word for them: he recognizes them as the wretched possessors of the "artistic temperament," with no creative output to give it vent and justify it. Like Beddoes, they feel themselves to be failures, but not in the same way or for the same reason. He knew his failure to be within him, and despaired of his own vocation. They believe the failure to be outside them, and despair of other men; they resent the world's refusal to recognize that vocation which to them is an inward certainty. They know, and continually assert, that they "have something there" which they desire to make manifest; but the manifestation is beyond their capacity. They are their own prisoners, languishing *incommunicado*.

Such men are dangerous; since Energy, if it cannot issue in creation, may contrive to burst its prison somehow and issue in its own opposite. The uncreative artist is the destroyer of all things, the active negation. When the Energy is not Christ, it is Antichrist, assuming leadership of the universe in the mad rush back to Chaos.

It is sometimes possible, when an Energy has been imprisoned and has issued violently in uncreation, to lead it back into creativeness and thus to restore it to harmony with the rest of its trinity. This is, or should be, the work of the psychiatrist, whose business it is to discover and unlock the prison-house, and to follow up

this psychoanalysis by establishing a psycho-synthesis of
creation. In the meantime, we may note the chaotic and
destructive tendency of much of that "surrealist" art
and literature which openly claims to derive its inspiration from the madhouse. The madhouse is a place of re-
straint; and the mad brain, essentially a cramped brain,
turning like a caged brute within the close circle of an
iron-bound logic. The common man (rightly) complains that this kind of art is unintelligible; it cannot be
otherwise, since the son is imprisoned and can only
whisper to his own imprisoned ghost. But the art itself
represents the prisoner's effort to escape; the danger is
lest he escape only into the activity of negation.[11]

Distinct from this total and perilous frustration, and
(mercifully) much more common, is partial and, as it
were, localized weakness in the sonhood, which assumes
innumerable forms, and from which no writer is absolutely free. *Every* failure in form and expression is a
failure in the son, from clichés and bad grammar to an
ill-constructed plot. It would be idle to try to enumerate
them all, but we may look at a few typical weaknesses.
The most striking and the most important for our purpose is perhaps the very common weakness which sets
the artist at odds with his material. This is a trouble
seated at the very heart of the sonhood, because the son
is *the* agent for the interpretation of the Idea in terms
of time-space-matter. The department of the writer's
job where this weakness shows most conspicuously is,
naturally enough, the theater, where the material factors

[11] The psychology of destruction and its connection with Surrealist Art has been studied by Dr. G. W. Pailthorpe.

that have to be handled are especially numerous, varied, and stubborn. So we will borrow a few illustrations from the drama.

We have already noticed [12] the mysterious difference between plays which are "good theater" and plays which are merely "good literature." We then attributed the playwright's failure to a general failure in love for the human and material medium in which he works. We may now inquire in more detail how this general failure corresponds to a failure in his trinity.

There may, I think, be two answers. The first concerns a failure of the ghost—the playwright has not been able to "sit in the theater" as he writes [13] and watch the effect of his work as a completed "response in Power." We shall come to this later on. But the second concerns a failure of the son—the playwright has not moved with his characters on the stage, and has, perhaps, actually forgotten the stage and the actors when working out his idea. Indeed, I have heard of playwrights who positively resented the presence of the players and the scenery as so many intrusive nuisances—necessary but tiresome obstructions which had to be negotiated, and whose very existence marred the beauties which they were called on to interpret. Now, actors and scenery are fully imbued with the general tiresomeness of all material things; in the random landslide to chaos they are particularly slippery and hard to check; and I suppose there is no good playwright from Æschylus to Noel Coward who has not, at various agitated moments, heartily wished his company in hades. This kind of tus-

[12] See p. 65 *sup.*
[13] See pp. 55 *sup.* and 170 *subt.*

sling and wrestling is all part of the creative game. But it is doubtful whether anybody ever yet wrote a good play who did not gladly think in terms of the stage while he was writing—who did not lovingly embrace the actress as well as the heroine, and who had not a lively affection for grease-paint and lath-and-plaster. The son works simultaneously in heaven and on earth; this needs to be unceasingly reaffirmed, artistically as well as theologically. He is in perpetual communion, both with the Father-Idea and with all matter. Not just with some particular sort of etherealized and refined matter—with things enskied and sainted—but with *all* matter; with flesh and blood and lath-and-plaster, as well as with words and thoughts. Accordingly, the playwright must keep his sonhood constantly and *simultaneously* active on two·planes and equally energetic on both. Let us suppose, for example, that he is writing a Nativity Play, and that he desires—a thing I would by no means advise, since the technical problems involved are very tricky—to show on the stage the appearance of the Angel to the watching shepherds. In his mind's eye he will doubtless have a vast and brilliant picture of "the real thing"; he will see the fields outside Bethlehem, with the little city in the distance and the domed sky over them, adorned with the Star of the Nativity as well as all the usual constellations. In the fields, there will be the shepherds and a herd of real sheep. And "lo" (that is, with an effect of overwhelming surprise) the Angel of the Lord "comes upon them," and "the glory of the Lord shines upon them." Imagination presents to him a form immense and lucid, probably wafted earthwards on rainbow wings, and bathed in the "light that never was on sea or land." That is all very well, and it is right that he should have that vision; but he is going to make trouble for himself and the producer if, having written: "Scene: Fields near Bethlehem; shepherds and sheep discovered. . . . Enter an Angel out of Heaven, in glory," he expects to see on the stage precisely what he saw in his mind. If he is not to suffer bitter disappointment he must see, while writing, *and at the same time as the vision*, the following mundane and material objects:

A wooden stage, perhaps 26ft. wide × 17ft. deep.

A painted sky-cloth or cyclorama, and a set of sky-borders.

A number of canvas flats and a ground-row; with some wooden rostrums.

A flock of hired or property sheep (and if he is wise, he will dismiss this horrid imagination at once, and substitute an effects-man to bleat "off").

Three actors or thereabouts, with appropriate wigs and costumes.

Another actor, of ordinary human stature, and weighing some 168 pounds of solid animal matter, draped in furniture satin, and supporting on his shoulders wings made of wood and paper (which are effective, but heavy) or gauze (which is light and transparent, but has an undignified tendency to wobble).

A rope to lower this unfortunate mummer, or a device which can open and reveal him suddenly at an appropriate height without displaying its mechanism to *any* part of the house (bearing in mind the

line of sight from the front row of the orchestra
and the back row of the gallery respectively).
Lighting equipment; comprising battens, spot-batten,
floats, floods, perches, movable and front-of-house
spots, and that exceedingly useful strength and stay
of all celestial phenomena known as an acting-area
flood; together with their gelatines, frosts and dim-
mers, and all possible combinations of all or any of
them that can be contrived in the average theater
without employing more than, say, two electricians
on the bridge and one on the spotboard.

I do not say that the playwright need be personally
acquainted with every mechanical trick in the stage-
manager's trade (though it will do him no harm if he
is); but unless he knows what can and what cannot be
done in the theater, the effect engineered for him by the
producer will probably be very unlike the effect he
hoped to see. Whereas, generally speaking, the more
closely he thinks in terms of flesh, and canvas, and elec-
tricity the more readily will the audience apprehend his
vision in terms of the light invisible. The glory of the
sonhood is manifest in the perfection of the flesh; and in
insisting on the perfect Manhood, theologians are labor-
ing no academic thesis, but one which is abundantly sup-
ported by theatrical experience.

In the case of our example, the reason is perfectly
clear. By working with the material means in mind, the
writer can so frame his words and action as to use all
the strength of the stage medium and avoid all its weaknesses; that is, he is enlisting on his side the theater's will
to creation. Oddly enough, for those who genuinely love

the stage, this business of working and thinking on two planes at once presents no difficulty of any kind; nor does the material vision, as might be supposed, impair or destroy the ideal vision. Both co-exist independently, and remain distinguishable. The stage set does not substitute itself for the imagined Bethlehem; and from those boundless pastures of the mind the visionary sheep are not banished.

I stress this matter, because the public mind is curiously confused about it. The playwright is frequently asked: "Doesn't it distress you to hear clumsy actors spoiling your beautiful lines?" If the actors really are clumsy and *do* spoil the lines, then distress is a mild term; but this is not what the questioner means. What he actually means is: "Don't you resent the intrusion of earthly and commonplace actors-as-such upon your spiritual fancies?" To ask the question is to insinuate that the playwright has mistaken his calling, since anybody who feels like that has no business on the working side of the stage-door. Such playwrights exist, but to be supposed one of them is no compliment. Those who take this view of the drama practice a kind of artistic Gnosticism—they consider that it is beneath the dignity of the son to dwell in a limited material body, and postulate for him a body which is a pure psychical manifestation, retaining all the supernatural qualities of the divinity.

Gnostic dramatists can produce very strange and absurd phenomena. St. John Ervine quotes an instance so sublime that it might be held incredible, if any human folly could be incredible:

I once read the manuscript of a five-act tragedy by a young author, which, apart from the time taken in changing the scenery, could have been acted in twenty minutes. The following is the whole of the second act:

The scene is a girl's room in a cottage. The room is in darkness: the heroine is in bed. She opens her eyes, she shuts her eyes: she clenches her hands and unclenches them: she tosses and turns, and then exclaims aloud:

Oh God! help me to be brave!

Curtain

The play was written by an adult who had written a good deal of poetry, and was, presumably, capable of exercising some judgment: but the account I have given of his play will indicate that, when he came to writing drama, he had no judgment at all. He evidently imagined that a great deal of time would be occupied by the "business" of the girl's agitation. But time on the stage is briefer than time in life.[14]

After discussing the question of the "time-illusion" in drama, the critic goes on:

There is another important point to be noted about this brief act, which is that, even if it could be adequately lengthened by pauses, by opening eyes and shutting eyes, clenching and unclenching fists, there would not be any point in all this business, for the simple reason that the entire scene is not only played in bed—where the scope for dramatic gestures is somewhat restricted—but in total darkness.[15]

And here we put our finger on the very nub of the matter. It is clear that the writer has not seen his stage

[14] St. John Ervine: *How to Write a Play.*
[15] *Loc. cit.*

at all—never even glanced at it, for if he had, he would have noticed at once that it was pitch dark. He has not looked upon his creation with the eyes of a man; he has looked only upon his ideal vision with the God's-eye of the author, which can see in darkness. The disregard of time and disregard of matter prove plainly that the failure is in the son, whose peculiar attribute is precisely to manifest the uncreate in matter and the timeless in time. It is noteworthy that the playwright "had written a good deal of poetry." The material body of "poetry," consisting as it does of the written or spoken word alone, is much less gross and much less complicated than the material body of drama. The critic does not mention whether the poetry was good poetry; in the absence of evidence to the contrary, we may presume that it was, and that the author's sonhood was adequate for this more tenuous manifestation, but not robust enough to deal with the great blocks of time and matter that have to be man-handled about the stage.

We shall notice that there is here also a weakness in the ghost, since the playwright was quite obviously not "sitting in the theater" at his own show. That is only to be expected. Any weakness in the son will inevitably affect the ghost. Indeed, if the creative artists had been called in to give evidence about the *filioque* clause, they must have come down heavily on the Western side of the controversy, since their experience leaves them in no doubt about the procession of the ghost from the son. Actually, however, our playwright was not lacking in response to his own Idea. One might say that, within "the heaven of his mind," the response was, if anything, over-powerful. He reacted strongly to the situation (whatever it was) and to the emotions that he had imagined for his heroine, but (because his son was not materially manifest), the response remained within him and could not be communicated socially in a Pentecost of power.

A bodiless Gnosticism is the besetting heresy of the "literary" dramatist and assumes many forms: such as, for example, the "literary" dialogue, which reads elegantly, but which no living actor can get his tongue round, and the "literary" stage-direction, which requires the actor to impart, by face and gesture, complicated states of mind or detailed bulletins of information which it would strain the combined resources of a Henry James and a Gibbon to compress into a paragraph. What the actor is required to practice is, in fact, a species of telepathy. The dramatic Gnostic has been ruthlessly pilloried for all time in Mr. Puff:

Lord Burleigh comes forward, shakes his head, and exits.

SNEER: He is very perfect indeed! Now, pray, what did he mean by that?
PUFF: You don't take it?
SNEER: No, I don't, upon my soul.
PUFF: Why, by that shake of the head, he gave you to understand that even though they had more justice in their cause, and wisdom in their measures—yet, if there was not a greater spirit shown on the part of the people, the country would at last fall a sacrifice to the hostile ambition of the Spanish monarchy.
SNEER: The devil! Did he mean all that by shaking his head?
PUFF: Every word of it—if he shook his head as I taught him.[16]

[16] Sheridan: *The Critic*, Act III.

Gnostic also is the preposterous stage-direction at the end of Elizabeth Barrett Browning's *Drama of Exile*. This is scarcely a fair example, since it is not likely that she ever seriously contemplated production on any commercial stage; but it is a rich pleasure to quote it:

The stars shine on brightly while ADAM *and* EVE *pursue their way into the far wilderness. There is a sound through the silence, as of the falling tears of an angel.*

"How much noise," inquires G. K. Chesterton with brutal common sense, "is made by an angel's tears? Is it a sound of emptied buckets, or of garden hoses, or of mountain cataracts?" That, unhappily, is just the sort of brutal question which a theatrical producer is obliged to ask. The "sound of a breaking harp-string" which brings down the curtain on *The Cherry Orchard* is a sufficiently queasy bit of "business"—but here at least, Tchekov's sonhood is stout enough to materialize into something definable.

It would be a fascinating entertainment to supply all the major Christological heresies with their artistic parallels. There is, for instance, artistic Arianism [17]—all technique and no vision, like the machine-made French bedroom comedies and that slicker and more mechanical kind of detective-story which is nothing but an arrangement of material clues. There are the propaganda writers—particularly the propaganda novelists and dramatists—Manichees,[18] whose son assumes what looks like a genuine human body, but is in fact a hollow simu-

---

[17] The heresy preached by Arius in the fourth century taught that Christ, though the noblest of all men, was not of the same substance as God the Father.—EDITOR'S NOTE.

[18] See page 95.

lacrum that cannot truly live, love or suffer, but only perform exemplary gestures symbolical of the Idea. There are the Patripassians, who involve the Father-Idea in the vicissitudes and torments of the creative Activity. Patripassian authors are those who (in the common phrase) "make it up as they go along"; serial writers are strongly tempted to this heresy.[19] We might, I think, also class as Patripassian those works in which the Idea insensibly undergoes a change in the course of writing, so that the cumulative effect of the whole thing when read is something other than the effect to which all its parts are supposed to be working. This peculiarity is a little difficult to convey clearly, but here is an example of it as noted by G. K. Chesterton, who (possibly because of his sound Trinitarian theology) is an exceptionally shrewd observer of scalene irregularities in other writers:

> Take the case of *In Memoriam*. . . . I will quote one verse . . . which has always seemed to me splendid, and which does express what the whole poem should express— but hardly does.
>
> > "That we may lift from out of dust
> > A voice as unto him that hears
> > A cry above the conquer'd years
> > To one that with us works, and trust—"

The poem should have been a cry above the conquered years. It might well have been that if the poet could have

---

[19] Patripassianism is the heresy which maintains that God the Father suffered on the cross with God the Son. Here it will be well to remind ourselves again that in our analogy "vicissitudes and torments" mean those which attend literary creation, and have nothing to do with the subject of the work or the emotions of the author's personal life.

said sharply at the end of it, as a pure piece of dogma, "I've forgotten every feature of the man's face: I know God holds him alive." But under the influence of the mere leisurely length of the thing, the reader *does* rather receive the impression that the wound has been healed only by time; that the victor hours *can* boast that this is the man that loved and lost, but all he was is overworn. This is not the truth; and Tennyson did not intend it for the truth. It is simply the result of the lack of something militant, dogmatic and structural in him: whereby he could not be trusted with the trail of a very long literary process without entangling himself like a kitten playing cats'-cradle.[20]

This curious literary result might be put forward as an example of father-weakness; but G. K. C. instinctively pigeon-holes it as a heretical imperfection in the son— "the lack of something *structural*," "the trail of a *long literary process*"—and I believe he is right: however it comes about it is Patripassianism.[21]

The drag of space and time must wrench us away from this enthralling sport of heresy-hunting. But we must say something about the third side of the Scalene Trinity—the imperfection of the ghost.

This, like everything to do with the ghost, is (for the reasons already given [22]) difficult to pin down for examination; which is unfortunate, seeing that failure in the

---

[20] G. K. Chesterton: *The Victorian Age in Literature.*

[21] On the other hand, the case of J. D. Beresford in *Writing Aloud* (see p. 70 *sq.*) is, I think, a Patripassianism deriving from father-weakness. The Idea was not sufficiently powerful in the writer's mind to control the Energy; so that the son, instead of "doing the will of the father" was doing his own will and that of the characters. Patripassianism must, in any case, imply a certain weakness in the father, since it is a heresy that denies and confounds the father's *persona.*

[22] Chapter VIII, *sup.*

ghost is more utterly and hopelessly disastrous than failure elsewhere—again, for the reasons given. For the
ghost is the medium in and by which both father and
son are creative, so that failure in this quarter is, of its
own nature, remediless. It may serve as a starting-point
to say that, whereas failure in the father may be roughly
summed up as a failure in Thought and failure in the
son as a failure in Action, failure in the ghost is a failure in Wisdom—not the wisdom of the brain, but the
more intimate and instinctive wisdom of the heart and
bowels. The unghosted are not unintelligent, nor yet
idle or unskilled; it is simply that there are certain things
which they do not know and seem incapable of knowing. Under the terms of our analogy, failure in the ghost
is the characteristic failure of the unliterary writer and
the inartistic artist. I do not mean the "natural," un-
trained artist as distinct from the bookish or academic
kind; I mean the men who use words without inspiration
and without sympathy. They may be compared to the
man who "has no feeling for" machinery; either he cannot make it work at all, or he wrenches and damages it
in the handling, or (worst of all) he irresponsibly sets it
going and turns it loose, without controlling it or noticing what has become of it. (It is, by the way, singularly
unfortunate that much of our social machinery, including the material machines themselves, has in these days
been given over into the hands of the unghosted.)

The unghosted writer is thus not only uninspired, but
also uncritical. The notion that self-criticism is necessarily a clog upon inspiration is quite erroneous, and is
honored only in the mind of the fifth-rate poetaster.
Creative criticism is the Spirit's continual response to its

own creation; the purely destructive and inhibiting kind of criticism being, like all destructive forces, merely the diabolic antitype of its divine archetype.

It is the deadness of the unghosted that hangs like a millstone upon the eloquence of pedestrian politicians and of conscientious parsons who have no gift for preaching. Words which should be living fall from their lips like stones, lacking the spirit of wisdom, which is the life. It is as though the speaker could not hear what he was saying—still less, hear himself with the ears of his listeners. The spirit is poured out neither in heaven nor in earth. In the theater of creation, the father sits aloof, insulated from contact; the son, like an automaton, exhibits a meaningless pattern of word and gesture; the seats are empty, and the dust-covers pulled over them.

What do you read, my lord?—Words, words, words.

A distressing trait of the unghosted is their complacency; they walk and talk, and do not know that they are dead. Neither, of course, are they alive to the deadness of their own creation. How should they be? Only the living can draw any distinction between death and life. Hence the lifeless sermons, the inanimate speeches, cumbered with the carcases of worn-out metaphor and flowers of rhetoric trampled to death; hence the movement into urgent battle of the embalmed mummies of sentiment, horsed like the dead Cid, and rigid in their grave-bands beneath the imposing panoply. Hence (more amusingly) those humorless juxtapositions of dead and living imagery which—to the astonished chagrin of the perpetrator—are hailed as mixed metaphor by the joyous and ribald ear of the live reader:

No doubt he has a hawk-like desire for action, without bridle and without saddle, across the Atlantic; [23]

the unfortunate verbal associations:

> The [something] torrent, leaping in the air,
> Left the astounded river's bottom bare; [24]

the unconscious blasphemies of the pious:

> That God from aye, to aye, may carry on
> Th' amazing work that HARRIS hath begun; [25]

hence also pomposity, pedestrianism, anti-climax, and those ill-timed "lines" in stage-plays which provoke laughter in the wrong place.

All this, indeed, comes back to that which is the very essence of the ghost's *persona:* the power to know good from evil.[26] It is the failure of this power which cuts off inspiration by cutting off contact with the father, who *is* the positive goodness in creation, and which destroys critical judgment by destroying the disjunction between negative and positive, between chaos and creation.

[23] *Ramsay MacDonald,* in a debate on Unemployment, 16.2.33. *Hansard,* Vol. 274, p. 1312.

[24] Some minor eighteenth-century poet, I think, on the subject of the Ark crossing Jordan. I have forgotten the reference, but the lapidary phrase itself is stamped indelibly on the memory.

[25] Jane Cave: *Poems on Various Subjects, Entertaining, Elegiac, and Religious,* 1783. J. C. Squire is the benefactor who has rescued this treasure from oblivion, *Life and Letters,* Art. "Jane Cave."

[26] In this context, of course, artistic good and evil; the unghosted of letters are frequently persons of a stiffly critical judgment in the sphere of morality.

XI

PROBLEM PICTURE

I am informed by philologists that the "rise to power" of these two words, "problem" and "solution" as the dominating terms of public debate, is an affair of the last two centuries, and especially of the nineteenth, having synchronised, so they say, with a parallel "rise to power" of the word "happiness"—for reasons which doubtless exist and would be interesting to discover. Like "happiness," our two terms "problem" and "solution" are not to be found in the Bible—a point which gives to that wonderful literature a singular charm and cogency. . . . On the whole, the influence of these words is malign, and becomes increasingly so. They have deluded poor men with Messianic expectations . . . which are fatal to steadfast persistence in good workmanship and to well-doing in general. . . . Let the valiant citizen never be ashamed to confess that he has no "solution of the social problem" to offer to his fellow-men. Let him offer them rather the service of his skill, his vigilance, his fortitude and his probity. For the matter in question is not, primarily, a "problem," nor the answer to it a "solution."
—L. P. JACKS: *Stevenson Lectures,* 1926-7

The aesthetic view of life is not, however, confined to those who can create or appreciate works of art. It exists wherever natural senses play freely on the manifold phenomena of our world, and when life as a consequence is found to be full of felicity.
—HERBERT READ: *Annals of Innocence and Experience*

PROBLEM PICTURE

SO far, we have been inquiring into the correspondence between the Christian Creeds and the experience of the artist on the subject of the creative mind and we have seen that there is, in fact, a striking agreement between them.

Now, how does all this concern the common man?

It has become abundantly clear of late years that something has gone seriously wrong with our conception of humanity and of humanity's proper attitude to the universe. We have begun to suspect that the purely analytical approach to phenomena is leading us only further and further into the abyss of disintegration and randomness, and that it is becoming urgently necessary to construct a synthesis of life. It is dimly apprehended that the creative artist does, somehow or other, specialize in construction, and also that the Christian religion does, in some way that is not altogether clear to us, claim to bring us into a right relation with a God whose attribute is creativeness. Accordingly, exhorted on all sides to become creative and constructive, the common man may reasonably turn to these two authorities, in the hope that they may shed some light, first, on what creativeness is, and, secondly, on its significance for the common man and his affairs.

Now we may approach this matter in two ways—from either end, so to speak. We may start from the artist himself, by observing that he has, in some way or other, got hold of a method of dealing with phenomena that is fruitful and satisfying to the needs of his personality. We may examine the workings of his mind when it is creatively engaged, and discover what is its intrinsic nature. Having done so, we may arrive at some conclusions about the nature of creative mind as such. And at this point we may set our conclusions over against those dogmatic pronouncements which the Church has made about the Creator, and discover that between the two there is a difference only of technical phraseology, and between the mind of the maker and the Mind of his Maker, a difference, not of category, but only of quality and degree.

Or we may begin with the Creeds alternatively, and ask what meaning for us, if any, is contained in this extraordinary set of formulae about Trinity-in-Unity, about the Eternal-Uncreate-Incomprehensible incarnate in space-time-matter, about the begotten Word and the Ghost proceeding, and about the orthodox God-Manhood so finickingly insisted upon and so obstinately maintained amid a dusty mêlée of mutually-contradictory heresies. We may take the statements to pieces, and translate them into the terms of an artistic analogy, only to discover that there then emerges a picture of the human artist at work—a picture exact to the minutest detail, familiar at every point, and corroborated in every feature by day-to-day experience. When we have done this, we may consider how strange and unexpected this must appear, if we hold it to be accidental. Obviously, it is not accidental. We may, of course, conclude that it is yet another instance of the rooted anthropomorphism of theologians. In seeking to establish the nature of the God they did not know, the Fathers of the Church began by examining the artist they did know, and constructed their portrait of Divinity upon that human model. Historically, of course, it is clear that they did not do this intentionally; nothing, I imagine, would be further from their conscious minds than to erect the Poet into a Godhead. But they may have done it unconsciously, proceeding from the human analogy, as human reasoning must. The theory is perfectly tenable. Let us, however, take note that if we hold this theory, we cannot, at the same time, hold that Trinitarian doctrine, as formulated, is obscure, apriorist and unrelated to human experience; since we are committed to supposing that it is a plain *a posteriori* induction *from* human experience.

On the other hand, we may conclude that the doctrine derives from a purely religious experience of God, as revealed in Christ and interpreted by abstract philosophic reasoning about the nature of the Absolute. In that case, we cannot call it irrational, however intricate and theoretical it may appear, since we have said it is a product of the reason. But if this theory, erected upon reason and religious experience, turns out to be capable of practical application in a totally different sphere of human experience, then we are forced to conclude also that the religious experience of Christianity is no isolated phenomenon; it has, to say the least of it, parallels elsewhere within the universe.

Now, when Isaac Newton observed a certain relationship and likeness between the behavior of the falling apple and that of the circling planets, it might be said with equal plausibility either that he argued by analogy from the apple to a theory of astronomy, or that while evolving a theory of astronomical mathematics he suddenly perceived its application to the apple. But it would scarcely be exact to say that, in the former case, he absurdly supposed the planets to be but apples of a larger growth, with seeds in them; or that, in the latter case, he had spun out a purely abstract piece of isolated cerebration which, oddly enough, turned out to be true about apples, though the movements of the planets themselves had no existence outside Newton's mathematics. Newton, being a rational man, concluded that the two kinds of behavior resembled each other—not because the planets had copied the apples or the apples copied the planets, but because both were examples of the working of one and the same principle. If you took a cross-section of the physical universe at the point marked "Solar System" and again at the point marked "Apple," the same pattern was exhibited; and the natural and proper conclusion was that this pattern was part of a universal structure, which ran through the world of visible phenomena as the grain runs through wood. Similarly, we may take a cross-section of the spiritual universe [1] at the point marked "Christian The-

---

[1] "Spiritual" is not quite the right word to oppose to "material"; nor yet is "vital" or "mental." Each is too limited, while "non-material" is too purely negative. As R. O. Kapp says (*op. cit.*), "we require a word which suggests that non-material reality possesses attributes lacking in matter"; and we require that this word shall cover the *whole* field of non-material reality. The word he suggests is "*diathetic*," meaning, "capable of disposing to a specification." Since this useful term is not yet common currency, we must make do with one of the others, intimating that we intend by it that which is purposive and orderly in its dealings with matter, as opposed to the random and chaotic habit of inanimate matter when left to itself.

ology" and at the point marked "Art," and find at both precisely the same pattern of the creative mind; it is open to us to draw a similar conclusion.

But if we do—if we conclude that creative mind is in fact the very grain of the spiritual universe—we cannot arbitrarily stop our investigations with the man who happens to work in stone, or paint, or music, or letters. We shall have to ask ourselves whether the same pattern is not also exhibited in the spiritual structure of every man and woman. And, if it is, whether, by confining the average man and woman to uncreative activities and an uncreative outlook, we are not doing violence to the very structure of our being. If so, it is a serious matter, since we have seen already the unhappy results of handling any material in a way that runs counter to the natural law of its structure.

It will at once be asked what is meant by asking the common man to deal with life creatively. We do not expect him to turn all his experience into masterpieces in ink or stone. His need is to express himself in agriculture or manufactures, in politics or finance, or in the construction of an ordered society. If he is required to be an "artist in living," the only image suggested by the phrase is that of a well-to-do person like Oscar Wilde, stretched in a leisured manner upon a sofa and esthetically contemplating the lilies of the field. The average man cannot afford this. Also, he supposes that the artist exercises complete mastery over his material. But the average man does not feel himself to be a complete master of life (which is *his* material). Far from it. To the average man, life presents itself, not as material malleable to his hand, but as a series of *problems* of extreme difficulty, which he has to *solve* with the means at his disposal. And he is distressed to find that the more means he can dispose of—such as machine-power, rapid transport, and general civilized amenities, the more his problems grow in hardness and complexity. This is particularly disconcerting to him, because he has been frequently told that the increase of scientific knowledge would give him "the mastery over nature"—which ought, surely, to imply mastery over life.

Perhaps the first thing that he can learn from the artist is that the only way of "mastering" one's material is to abandon the whole conception of mastery and to co-operate with it in love: whosoever will be a lord of life, let him be its servant. If he tries to wrest life out of its true nature, it will revenge itself in judgment, as the work revenges itself upon the domineering artist.

The second thing is, that the words "problem" and "solution," as commonly used, belong to the analytic approach to phenomena, and not to the creative. Though it has become a commonplace of platform rhetoric that we can "solve our problems" only by dealing with them "in a creative way," those phrases betray, either that the speaker has repeated a popular cliché without bothering to think what it means, or that he is quite ignorant of the nature of creativeness.

From our brief study of the human maker's way of creation, it should be fairly clear that the creator does not set out from a set of data, and proceed, like a crossword solver or a student of elementary algebra, to deduce from them a result which shall be final, predictable, complete and the only one possible. The concept of "problem and solution" is as meaningless, applied to the act of creation, as it is when applied to the act of pro-creation. To add John to Mary in a procreative process does not produce a "solution" of John's and Mary's combined problem; it produces George or Susan, who (in addition to being a complicating factor in the life of his or her parents) possesses an independent personality with an entirely new set of problems. Even if, in the manner of the sentimental novel of the 'nineties, we allow the touch of baby hands to loosen some of the knots into which John and Mary have tied themselves, the "solution" (meaning George or Susan) is not the only one possible, nor is it final, predictable or complete.

Again, there is no strictly mathematical or detective-story sense in which it can be said that the works of a poet are the "solution" of the age in which he lived; indeed, it is seldom at all clear which of these two factors is the result of the other. Much breath and ink are continually expended in the effort to find out, under the impression that this also is a "problem" awaiting a final, predictable, complete and sole possible "solution." The most one can say is that between the poet and his age there is an intimate connection of mutual influence, highly complex and various, and working in all directions of time and space.

Yet the common man, obsessed by the practice of a mathematical and scientific period, is nevertheless obscurely aware that that enigmatic figure, the creative artist, possesses some power of interpretation which he has not, some access to the hidden things behind that baffling curtain of phenomena which he cannot penetrate. Sometimes he merely resents this, as men do often resent an inexplicable and incommunicable superiority.

Sometimes he dismisses it: "He is a dreamer, let us leave him. Pass." But at other times—especially when the disharmonies of contemporary existence force themselves on his attention with an urgency that cannot be ignored, he will lay hold of the artist and demand to be let into his secret. "Here, you!" he will cry, "you have some trick, some pass-word, some magic formula that unlocks the puzzle of the universe. Apply it for us. Give us the solution to the problems of civilization."

This, though excusable, is scarcely fair, since the artist does not see life as a problem to be solved, but as a medium for creation. He is asked to settle the common man's affairs for him; but he is well aware that creation settles nothing. The thing that is settled is finished and dead, and his concern is not with death but with life: "that ye may have life and have it more abundantly." True, the artist can, out of his own experience, tell the common man a great deal about the fulfillment of man's nature in living; but he can produce only the most unsatisfactory kind of reply if he is persistently asked the wrong question. And, as I have (perhaps somewhat heatedly) maintained in my preface, an incapacity for asking the right question has grown, in our time and country, to the proportions of an endemic disease.

The desire of being persuaded that all human experience may be presented in terms of a problem having a predictable, final, complete and sole possible solution accounts, to a great extent, for the late extraordinary popularity of detective fiction. This, we feel, is the concept of life which we want the artist to show us. It is significant that readers should so often welcome the detective-story as a way of escape from the problems of existence.

It "takes their minds off their troubles." Of course it does; for it softly persuades them that love and hatred, poverty and unemployment, finance and international politics, are problems capable of being dealt with and solved in the same manner as the Death in the Library. The beautiful finality with which the curtain rings down on the close of the investigation conceals from the reader that no part of the "problem" has been "solved" *except that part which was presented in problematic terms.* The murderer's motive has been detected, but nothing at all has been said about the healing of his murderous soul. Indeed, a major technical necessity of the writing is to prevent this aspect of the matter from ever presenting itself to the reader's mind. (For if we know too much about the murderer's soul beforehand, we shall anticipate the solution, and if we sympathize with him too much after discovery, we shall resent his exposure and condemnation. If sympathy cannot be avoided, the author is at pains, either to let the criminal escape or to arrange for his suicide, and so transfer the whole awkward business to a higher tribunal, whose decisions are not openly promulgated.)

Since, as I have already explained, I am more intimately acquainted with my own works than with other people's, may I illustrate this point from the novel *Gaudy Night.* This contains three parallel problems, one solved, one partially solved, and the third insoluble. All three are related to the same *theme,* which is the "Father-Idea" of the book.

The first problem is presented in purely problematical terms: "Who caused the disturbances at Shrewsbury College, and why?" This is solved, within the terms in which it was set, by the predictable, final, complete and sole possible answer: "The culprit was the maid Annie; and her motive was revenge for an act of justice meted out against her husband by a certain academic woman in the interests of professional integrity."

The second "problem" is not really a problem at all: it is a human perplexity: "How are Peter and Harriet to retrieve their relationship from a false emotional situation into which it has been forced by a series of faults on both sides?" Here, by an exercise on both sides of a strict intellectual integrity, that situation is so modified that they are enabled to enter into a new relationship, presenting fresh situations with the prospect of further errors and misunderstandings. This "solution" is neither final nor complete; and though it is both predictable and necessary under the law of the book's nature as an artistic structure it is neither so far as the general law of nature is concerned.

The third "problem" (if one likes to call it so) is presented, both to the reader and to the academic woman who carried out the act of justice on Annie's husband, in terms of a confrontation of values: Is professional integrity so important that its preservation must override every consideration of the emotional and material consequences? To this moral problem no solution is offered, except in terms of situation and character. Argument on both sides is presented; but judgment is pronounced only in the form: Here are this life and that life, these standards and those standards, these people and those people, locked in a conflict which cannot but be catastrophic. Wherever the quality of experience is enriched,

there is life. The only judgment this book can offer you
is the book itself.

The enriching (and also catastrophic) quality of Integrity is thus the Father-Idea of the book, providing
the mechanics of the detective problem, the catalyst that
precipitates the instability of the emotional situation,
and also a theme which unites the microcosm of the
book to the macrocosm of the universe. I have dealt
with this story at rather egotistical length because of a
criticism made by one intelligent reader, also a writer of
detective fiction. He said:

"Why do you allow the academic woman to have
any doubts that she pursued the right course with
Annie's husband? She seems to think she may have been
wrong. Doesn't that conflict with your whole thesis?"

What is obvious here is the firmly implanted notion
that all human situations are "problems" like detective
problems, capable of a single, necessary, and categorical
solution, which must be wholly right, while all others
are wholly wrong. But this they cannot be, since human
situations are subject to the law of human nature, whose
evil is at all times rooted in its good, and whose good
can only redeem, but not abolish, its evil. The good that
emerges from a conflict of values cannot arise from the
total condemnation or destruction of one set of values,
but only from the building of a new value, sustained,
like an arch, by the tension of the original two. We do
not, that is, merely examine the data to disentangle something that was in them already: we use them to construct something that was not there before: neither cir-
cumcision nor uncircumcision, but a new creature.

The artist's "new creature" is not a moral judgment

but his work of living art. If the common man asks the artist for help in producing moral judgments or practical solutions, the only answer he can get is something like this: You must learn to handle practical situations as I handle the material of my book: you must take them and use them to *make a new thing*. As A. D. Lindsay puts it:

In the morality of my station and duties [*i.e. of the moral code*] the station presents us with the duty, and we say "Yes" or "No." "I will" or "I will not." We choose between obeying or disobeying a given command. In the morality of challenge or grace the situation says, "Here is a mess, a crying evil, a need! What can you do about it?" We are asked not to say "Yes" or "No" or "I will" or "I will not," but to be inventive, to create, to discover something new. The difference between ordinary people and saints is not that saints fulfil the plain duties which ordinary men neglect. The things saints do have not usually occurred to ordinary people at all. . . . "Gracious" conduct is somehow like the work of an artist. It needs imagination and spontaneity. It is not a choice between presented alternatives but the creation of something new.[2]

The distinction between the artist and the man who is not an artist thus lies in the fact that the artist is living in the "way of grace," so far as his vocation is concerned. He is not necessarily an artist in handling his personal life, but (since life is the material of his work) he has at least got thus far, that he is using life to make something new. Because of this, the pains and sorrows of this troublesome world can never, for him, be *wholly* meaningless and useless, as they are to the man who dumbly endures them and can (as he complains with

[2] A. D. Lindsay: *The Two Moralities.*

only too much truth) "make nothing of them." If,
therefore, we are to deal with our "problems" in "a creative way," we must deal with them along the artist's
lines: not expecting to "solve" them by a detective trick,
but to "make something of them," even when they are,
strictly speaking, insoluble.

I do not say that it is *impossible* to view all human
activity, even the activity of the artist, in terms of
"problem and solution." But I say that, however we use
the words, they are wholly inadequate to the reality
they are meant to express. We can think of Shakespeare,
setting himself to solve the problem of *Hamlet:* that is,
the problem of producing a reasonably "box-office" play
from the recalcitrant material bequeathed to him by
earlier dramatists. Or we can think of him solving in-
cidental problems of production—e.g., how to arrange
his scenes so as to give those actors who were doubling
two parts time to change, without introducing "pad-
ding" into the dialogue. We can think of him solving
the problem of Hamlet's character: how to reconcile,
plausibly, his delay in revenging his father with his
swiftness in disposing of Rosencrantz and Guildenstern.
But when we have solved all the *Hamlet* problems that
puzzle the critics, we are no nearer to laying hold on the
essential thing—the Idea and the Energy that make
Hamlet a living power. *Hamlet* is something more than
the sum of its problems. We can see St. Paul's Cathedral
purely in terms of the problems solved by the architect
—the calculations of stress and strain imposed by the re-
quirements of the site. But there is nothing there that
will tell us why men were willing to risk death to save
St. Paul's from destruction; or why the bomb that

crashed through its roof was felt by millions like a blow over the heart.

All human achievements *can* be looked on as problems solved—particularly in retrospect, because, if the work has been well done, the result will then appear inevitable. It seems as though *this* was the only "right" way, predestined and inevitable from the start. So it is the "right" way, in the sense that it is the way which agrees with the maker's Father-Idea. But there was no inevitability about the Idea itself.

It is here that we begin to see how the careless use of the words "problem" and "solution" can betray us into habits of thought that are not merely inadequate but false. It leads us to consider all vital activities in terms of a particular *kind* of problem, namely the kind we associate with elementary mathematics and detective fiction. These latter are "problems" which really can be "solved" in a very strict and limited sense, and I think the words "problem" and "solution" should be reserved for these special cases. Applied indiscriminately, they are fast becoming a deadly danger. They falsify our apprehension of life as disastrously as they falsify our apprehension of art. At the cost of a little recapitulation, I should like to make this quite clear.

There are four characteristics of the mathematical or detective problem which are absent from the "life-problem"; but because we are accustomed to find them in the one, we look for them in the other, and experience a sense of frustration and resentment when we do not find them.

1. *The detective problem is always soluble.* It is, in fact, constructed for the express purpose of being

solved, and when the solution is found, the problem no longer exists. A detective or mathematical problem that could not be solved by *any* means at all, would simply not be what we understand by a "problem" in this sense. But it is unwise to suppose that all human experiences present problems of this kind. There is one vast human experience that confronts us so formidably that we cannot pretend to overlook it. There is no solution to death. There is no means whatever whereby you or I, by taking thought, can solve this difficulty in such a manner that it no longer exists. From very early days, alchemists have sought for the elixir of life, so reluctant is man to concede that there can be any problem incapable of solution. And of late, we note a growing resentment and exasperation in the face of death. We do not so much fear the pains of dying, as feel affronted by the notion that anything in this world should be inevitable. Our efforts are not directed, like those of the saint or the poet, to make something creative out of the idea of death, but rather to seeing whether we cannot somehow evade, abolish, and, in fact, "solve the problem" of death. The spiritual and mental energy which we expend upon resenting the inevitability of death is as much wasted as that which we from time to time have expended on attempts to "solve the problem" of perpetual motion.

Further, this irrational preoccupation curiously hampers us in dealing with such a practical question as that of the possibility of war. It encourages us to look on the evil of war as consisting, first and foremost, in the fact that it kills a great many people. If we concentrate on this, instead of thinking of it in terms of the havoc it plays with the lives and souls of the survivors, we shall direct all our efforts to evading war at all costs, rather than to dealing intelligently with the conditions of life which cause wars and are caused by wars. This, in fact, is precisely what we did in 1919-1939.

We did not, of course, really believe that, if only we could evade war, we should evade death altogether. We only talked and behaved as though we thought so. Death is less noticeable when it occurs privately and piecemeal. In time of peace we can pretend, almost successfully, that it is only a regrettable accident, which ought to have been avoided. If a wealthy old gentleman of ninety-two suddenly falls dead of heart-failure, the papers headline the event: "Tragic Death of Millionaire"; and we feel quite astonished and indignant that anybody so rich should be cut off in his prime. With all that money available for research, science should have been able to solve the problem of death for him. If we do not think this, then why use the word "tragic" about a death so clean, painless, and mature? (Do not say that the headline is too foolish to be true: I saw it with my own eyes.)

We said last time that we hated war because it killed the young and strong before their time. But we are just as angry this time to see the old and the infirm perish with the rest. No man can die more than once; but great disasters, great pestilences, and above all great wars, cram our eyes and ears with the detested knowledge that life intends to kill us.

Because of that, we would not risk war, for right or justice, or even in the hope of preserving peace. We threw down our arms, crying, "No More War!", and so delivered up Europe.

Yet we know perfectly well that the paradox "he that will lose his life shall save it" is a plain and practical fact. Unless we are willing to risk death by jumping from a burning house, we shall most certainly be burnt to death. Indeed, had not the will of our physical nature been ready to accept death, we could never have been born.

The "problem of death" is not susceptible of detective-story solution. The only two things we can do with death are, first: to postpone it, which is only partial solution, and, secondly, to transfer the whole set of values connected with death to another sphere of action—that is, from time to eternity.

This brings us to consider the next two characteristics of the detective problem:

2. *The detective problem is completely soluble:* no loose ends or unsatisfactory enigmas are left anywhere. The solution provides for everything and every question that is asked is answered. We are not left with a balance of probabilities in favor of one conclusion or another; nor does the fixing of the crime on the butler involve the detective in fresh enigmas connected with the cook. Such uncertainties may appear to arise in the course of the story, but they are all cleared up in the end by the discovering of the complete solution. It should not be necessary to point out here that this happy result proceeds from the simple fact that the author has been careful not to ask the questions that the solution will not answer.

Now, our tendency to look for this kind of complete

solution without lacunae or compensatory drawbacks badly distorts our view of a number of activities in real life. Medicine is a good example. We are inclined to think of health in terms of disease and cure. Here on the one hand is (we think) one definite disease, and there, on the other hand, should be the one, definite and complete "cure." Apply the cure to the disease, and the result ought to be an exact "solution" of the "problem" presented. If the physician cannot name the disease on sight and immediately produce the prescribed cure, we feel resentfully that the man does not know his business.

In the same way, there used to be a firmly-rooted belief that to every poison there existed "the antidote"—a benevolent drug which would exactly reverse, each by each, the effects of the original poison and restore the body to the *status quo ante*. There are in fact, I believe, only two drugs which are complementary in this way, atropine and physostigmine [3] (incidentally, neither of them is "benevolent"—both are deadly poisons). With other drugs which are used to counteract one another, the reversal of the effects is only partial, or is rather a counteraction of the symptoms than a healing of the mischief done to the organs. In most cases, the usefulness of the curative drug is only to hold off or mitigate the effects of the poison until the body can summon its physical resources to cure itself. In certain instances, one disease can be got rid of only at the cost of contracting another, as in the malaria treatment of syphilis. Or the treatment demanded by—let us say—a diseased condition of the lungs may be impossible for one particular pa-

[3] Dixon Mann: *Forensic Medicine:* Art. "Antagonism of Poisons."

tient, because his constitution could not stand its violent effects upon the heart.

We have, perhaps, abandoned the superstitious belief in antidotes; but we continue to hug the delusion that all ill-health is caused by some single, definite disease, for which there ought to be a single, definite and complete cure without unfortunate after-effects. We think of our illness as a kind of cross-word *of which the answer is known to somebody:* the complete solution must be *there,* somewhere; it is the doctor's business to discover and apply it.

But the physician is not solving a cross-word: he is performing a delicate, adventurous, and experimental creative act, of which the patient's body is the material, and to which the creative co-operation of the patient's will is necessary. He is not rediscovering a state of health, temporarily obscured; he is remaking it, or rather, helping it to remake itself. This may indeed be looked upon as a problem; but it is not the same kind of problem as that presented by those in the algebra-book: "If a cistern is filled by pipes A and B in 25 and 32 minutes respectively"; and the answer is not likely to be so precise or to cover all the conditions so satisfactorily.

The patient's best way to health and peace of mind is to enter with understanding into the nature of the physician's task. If he does so, he will not only be better placed to co-operate creatively with him, but he will be relieved from the mental misery of impatience and frustration.

We may note, at the moment of writing, a similar kind of misconception about "the problem of the night

bomber." The agony of our impatience with these horrid intrusions is only increased by imagining that "the
solution" already exists somewhere or other and that
nothing but the criminal folly and sloth of the authorities prevents it from being immediately discovered and
applied. We shall feel better about the business if we
scrap the whole misleading notion and think instead:
"Now a new thing has to be made that has never been
made before." It is not to detectives that we have to
look for help, but to inventors—to the men of creative
ideas. And by this time we know something of the way
in which creative work is done.

"We are at work now upon various devices," says
some harassed spokesman; and the imagination sees "us"
industriously assembling the device, as though it had
been delivered in parts from a celestial workshop, and
had only to be fitted together according to the book of
instructions and put into use the same evening. That is
not creation's method. There is the wayward, the un-
predictable, the not-to-be-commanded Idea, which may
make its presence felt in the mind after long hours of
fruitless thought and work, or suddenly after no
thought at all, or after a long fallow period of uncon-
sciousness, during which the conscious has been otherwise employed, but always in a day and an hour which
we know not. There is the long, bitter, baffled struggle
of the Energy, calculating, designing, experimenting,
eliminating error, resisting the slide into randomness; the
first manifestation of the Idea in a model made with
hands; the renewed labor of the Activity, testing, improving, unbuilding error to rebuild nearer to the
Idea; the new model made with hands and re-checked,

re-tested; the labor of a manifold Activity in the shops to multiply the image of the Idea and distribute it in space; the communication of the Idea in Power to the men who have to understand and use the device. After all of which, if the Idea is a true and powerful Idea, it can at length produce its final manifestation in Power, and bring, as we say, results. And even then, the result may not be a single and complete "answer to the problem"; because this problem is not like a cipher, which carries within itself the material for its own decoding. Very likely there may be no one conclusive "answer" to the night-bomber.

Another kind of inconclusive "problem" presents itself when we desire to enjoy, simultaneously and completely, two mutually incompatible things: such, for example, as liberty and order, or liberty and equality. I have discussed these elsewhere,[4] and will add here only the brief reminder that individual liberty is compatible with social order only if the individual freely consents to restrictions on his personal liberty; and that if every man is free to develop all his powers equally to the utmost, there can be no sort of equality between the weak and the strong. Again, there is the hopeless dilemma that confronts every attempt to establish a Kingdom of God on earth: "Goodness, armed with power, is corrupted; and pure love without power is destroyed."[5] Such "problems" cannot be solved mathematically: there is no single solution that is wholly right: Either there must be compromise, or the situation must be considered again in other terms, for in the terms in which it is set,

[4] *Begin Here:* Chapter 2.
[5] Reinhold Niebuhr: *Beyond Tragedy.*

the problem is insoluble. This brings us to our third point.

3. *The detective problem is solved in the same terms in which it is set.* Here is one of the most striking differences between the detective problem and the work of the creative imagination. The detective problem is deliberately set in such a manner that it can be solved without stepping outside its terms of reference. This is part of its nature as a literary form, and the symmetry of this result constitutes a great part of its charm. Does not an initiate-member of the Detection Club swear to observe this entirely arbitrary rule?

PRESIDENT: Do you promise that your Detectives shall well and truly detect the Crimes presented to them, using those Wits which it shall please you to bestow upon them and not placing reliance upon, nor making use of, Divine Revelation, Feminine Intuition, Mumbo-Jumbo, Jiggery-Pokery, Coincidence or the Act of God?

CANDIDATE: I do.

But life is no candidate for the Detection Club. It makes unabashed use of all the forbidden aids (not excepting Mumbo-Jumbo and Jiggery-Pokery); and frequently sets its problems in terms which *must* be altered if the problem is to be solved at all.

Take, for example, the problem of Unemployment. Have we perhaps so far failed to solve it because of the terms in which we have chosen to set it? In the terms in which it is set, it is an economic problem, concerned with such matters as the proper balance between Labor and Capital, Hours and Wages, Property and Financial Returns. When tackled along these lines, it disconcerts us by producing as offshoots all manner of confusing and contradictory questions; such as: Should wages be adjusted to the time worked, or to the amount and quality of the work done, or to the needs of the worker? At this point, we begin to notice irrelevancies and discrepancies, as though our detective-story had stepped outside its allotted terms of reference. We notice also that the "Problem of Unemployment" limits us to the consideration of Employment only; it does not allow us even to consider the Work itself—whether it is worth doing or not, or whether the workman is to find satisfaction in doing the work, or only in the fact of being employed and receiving his pay-envelope. We may then ask ourselves: Should a man work in order to get enough money to enable him to cease from working, or should he desire only such payment as will enable him to live in order to carry on his work? If the former is true, then blessed are the rich, for they are the flower of a leisured civilization; but, if the latter is true, then blessed is the worker who gets no more than a living wage. When we have got so far, we may begin to suspect that the "problem of Unemployment" is not soluble in the terms in which it is set; and that what we ought to be asking is a totally different set of questions about Work and Money. Why, for example, does the actor so eagerly live to work, while the factory-worker, though often far better paid, reluctantly works to live? How much money would men need, beyond the subsistence that enables them to continue working, if the world (that is, you and I) admired work more than wealth? Does the fact that he is employed fully compensate a man for the fact that his work is trivial, unnecessary, or positively harmful to society: the manufacture of imbecile and ugly ornaments, for instance, or the deliberate throat-cutting between rival manufacturers of the same commodity? Ought we, in fact, to consider whether work is worth doing, before we encourage it for the sake of employment? In deciding whether man should be employed at a high wage in the production of debased and debasing cinema films or at a lower wage in the building of roads and houses, ought we to think *at all* about the comparative worth and necessity of bad films and good houses? Has the fact that enthusiastic crowds cheer and scream around professional footballers, while offering no enthusiastic greetings to longshoremen, anything to do with the wages offered to footballers and longshoremen respectively?

When we have ceased to think of work and money in the purely economic terms implied by "the Problem of Unemployment," then we are on our way to thinking in terms of creative citizenship, for we shall be beginning to make something with our minds—instead of "solving a problem" we shall be creating a new way of life.[6]

"Whose, therefore, shall she be in the Resurrection? for the seven had her to wife." In the terms in which you set it, the problem is unanswerable; but in the Kingdom of Heaven, those terms do not apply. You have asked the question in a form that is much too limited; the "solution" must be brought in from outside your sphere of reference altogether.

4. *The detective problem is finite;* when it is solved,

[6] See Postscript at end of this chapter.

there is an end of it—or, as George Joseph Smith casu-
ally observed concerning the brides he had drowned in
their baths, "When they are dead, they are done with."
The detective problem summons us to the energetic
exercise of our wits precisely in order that, when we
have read the last page, we may sit back in our chairs
and cease thinking. So does the cross-word. So does
the chess-problem. So does the problem about A, B,
and C building a wall. The struggle is over and finished
with and now we may legitimately, if we like, cease
upon the midnight with no pain. The problem leaves us
feeling like that because it is deliberately designed to
do so. Because we can, in this world, achieve so little,
and so little perfectly, we are prepared to pay good
money in order to acquire a vicarious sensation of
achievement. The detective-novelist knows this, and so
do the setters of puzzles. And the schoolboy, triumphantly scoring a line beneath his finished homework,
is thankful that he need not, in the manner so disquiet-
ingly outlined by Professor Leacock, inquire into the
subsequent history of A, B, and C.

But this is the measure, not of the likeness between
problems in detection and problems in life, but of the
unlikeness. For the converse is also true; when they are
done with, they are dead.[7] Consider how, in the last

[7] [Utopian theory] imagines that perfect innocency, a new childhood, lies at the end of the social process. It thinks itself capable of
creating a society in which all tensions are resolved and the final
root of human anarchy is eliminated. If that were really possible its
new society would not be the beginning of history, as it fondly
imagines, but its end. . . . The problem of good and evil cannot be
completely resolved in history.—Reinhold Niebuhr: *Beyond Tragedy*.
The random "shaking down" of inanimate matter acts to produce
states of increasing stability, and may be expected to reach a final

twenty years, we have endeavored to deal with the "problem of peace and security," and whether we do not still secretly hug the delusion that it is possible to deal with it as a "problem." We really persuaded ourselves that peace was something that could be achieved by a device, by a set of regulations, by a League of Nations or some other form of constitution, that would "solve" the whole matter once and for all. We continue to delude ourselves into the belief that "when the war is over" we shall "this time" discover the trick, the magic formula, that will stop the sun in heaven, arrest the course of events, make further exertion unnecessary. Last time we failed to achieve this end—and why? Chiefly because we supposed it to be achievable. Because we looked at peace and security as a problem to be solved and not as a work to be made.

Now the artist does not behave like this. He may finish a book, as we may finish a war or set up the machinery of a League, and he may think it is very good and allow his Energy a brief sabbath of repose. But he knows very well that this is only a pause in the unending labor of creation. He does not subscribe to the heresy that confounds his Energy with his Idea, and the Son's brief sabbath in time with the perpetual sabbaths of the Trinity in Heaven. For the thing he has made is a living thing, and it is not sterile. It continually proliferates new themes and new fancies, and new occasions for thought and action. Each chapter concluded is only

state in which stability is complete and no further development possible. When, in the presence of life, matter is built into ordered pattern, it is maintained there only in a state of instability or tension. Thus, in the universe as we know it, the will to stability is the will to death.

a day's end in the course of the book; each book concluded is only a year's end in the course of a life's pilgrimage. Or, if you like the metaphor better, it is a "still" cut out and thrown off from the endless living picture which his creative mind reels out. It is a picture in itself, but it leads only from the picture behind it to the picture in front of it, as part of a connected process.

This the artist knows, though the knowledge may not always stands in the forefront of his consciousness. At the day's end or the year's end he may tell himself: the work is done. But he knows in his heart that it is not, and that the passion of making will seize him again the following day and drive him to construct a fresh world. And though he may imagine for the moment that this fresh world is wholly unconnected with the world he has just finished, yet, if he looks back along the sequence of his creatures, he will find that each was in some way the outcome and fulfillment of the rest—that all his worlds belong to the one universe that is the image of his own Idea. I know it is no accident that *Gaudy Night*, coming towards the end of a long development in detective fiction, should be a manifestation of precisely the same theme as the play *The Zeal of Thy House*, which followed it and was the first of a series of creatures embodying a Christian theology. They are variations upon a hymn to the Master Maker; and now, after nearly twenty years, I can hear in *Whose Body?* the notes of that tune sounding unmistakably under the tripping melody of a very different descant; and further back still, I hear it again, in a youthful set of stanzas in *Catholic Tales:*

> I make the wonderful carven beams
> Of cedar and of oak
> To build King Solomon's house of dreams
> With many a hammer-stroke,
> And the gilded, wide-winged cherubims.
>
> I have no thought in my heart but this:
> How bright will be my bower
> When all is finished; My joy it is
> To see each perfect flower
> Curve itself up to the tool's harsh kiss.
>
> How shall I end the thing I planned?
> Such knots are in the wood!
> With quivering limbs I stoop and stand,
> My sweat runs down like blood—
> I have driven the chisel through My hand.

I should not write it quite like that today—at least, I hope I should avoid the bright bower and the quivering limbs and the exclamation-mark in the last verse. But the end is clearly there in the beginning. It would not be quite exact to say that the wheel has come full circle, or even, in the image that the time-students have made fashionable, that the spiral has made another turn over its starting-point. The Idea was from the beginning in every corner of the universe which it contains, and eternally begets its manifestations. There is never any point in time that can conclude or comprehend the Idea. The problem is never so solved that it is abolished: but each time it is restated, a new thing is made and signed with the formula "Q.E.F." [8]

The desire to solve a living problem by a definitive

[8] *Quod erat faciendum:* Which was to be done.—EDITOR'S NOTE.

and sterile conclusion is natural enough: it is part of the material will to death. It is bred in the bones of the most enlightened and "progressive" of mankind, who hate it when they see it in others, not realizing that what appears to them to be a detestable stranger is in fact their own face in a mirror.

The man who uses violent invective against those who seek to "uphold the *status quo*" or cling to an "outworn tradition," is justified in doing so *only* if he himself contemplates no fixed point of achievement ahead. If he thinks within himself, "after the war," or "after the revolution," or "after the Federation of Europe," or "after the triumph of the proletariat," the problem will be solved, then he is no better than they are. And he is horribly deluding both himself and others—the blind leading the blind into a blind alley. In fact, by saying or thinking any such thing, he is establishing precisely the conditions which make any approach to achievement impossible.

When we examine these four characteristics of the detective problem, we begin to see why it is so easy to look upon all the phenomena of life in terms of "problem and solution," and also why the "solution" is so seldom satisfactory, even when we think we have reached it. For in order to persuade ourselves that we can "solve" life, we have only to define it in terms which admit of solution. Unless we do this, not only the solution but the problem itself is unintelligible. Take any phenomenon you like: Take a rose. How will you proceed to solve a rose? You can cultivate roses, smell them, gather and wear them, make them into perfume or potpourri, paint them or write poetry about them; these are all creative activities. But can you solve roses? Has that expression any meaning? Only if you first define the rose in terms which presuppose the answer. You can say: If the rose is regarded as an arrangement of certain chemical components, then the chemical formula for the rose is x. Or you can say: If the rose is regarded geometrically as a complex system of plane surfaces, then the formula for *this* rose is so-and-so. Or you can say: If the rose is regarded as an example of the Mendelian heredity of color-variations, then the method for cultivating blue roses is as follows. But none of these answers is going to solve the rose; and if the first is complete and final for the chemist, it remains altogether inadequate for the woman putting roses in a vase; and if the second may give some assistance to the painter, it leaves the gardener dissatisfied; while the third is probably undiscoverable, and, even if it were not, would do nothing to help the perfumer. Yet the perfumer, the gardener, the woman and the painter, being occupied with the rose itself and not with its solution, can all present the world with new manifestations of the rose, and by so doing communicate the rose to one another in power.

The danger of speaking about life exclusively in terms of problem and solution is that we are thus tempted to overlook the limitations of this detective game and the very existence of the initial arbitrary rule that makes the playing of it possible. The rule is to exclude from the terms of the problem everything that the solution cannot solve. It is diverting and useful to know that, for the chemist, a man is made up of a few pennyworth of salt, sugar, iron and what not, together with an intolerable deal of water. But we must not assert that, "Man is, in fact, nothing but" these things, or suppose that the solution of the pennyworths in the water will produce a complete and final solution of man. For this means that we have forgotten the qualification "for the chemist." That qualification reduces our assertion to the more limited form: "If man is nothing but a chemical, this is his chemical formula"—a very different matter. Somewhat similarly, the popular game of debunking great men usually proceeds by excluding their insoluble greatness from the terms of the problem and presenting a watery solution of the remainder; but this is, by definition, no solution of the man or of his greatness.

It was said by Kronecker, the mathematician: "God made the integers; all else is the work of man." Man can table the integers and arrange them into problems which he can solve in the terms in which they are set. But before the inscrutable mystery of the integers themselves he is helpless, unless he calls upon that Tri-Unity in himself which is made in the image of God, and can include and create the integers.

This is the vocation of the creative mind in man. The mind in the act of creation is thus not concerned to solve problems within the limits imposed by the terms in which they are set, but to fashion a synthesis which includes the whole dialectics of the situation in a manifestation of power. In other words, the creative artist, as such, deals, not with the working of the syllogism, but with that universal statement which forms its major premise. That is why he is always a disturbing influence; for all logical argument depends upon acceptance of the major premise, and this, by its nature, is not susceptible of logical proof. The hand of the creative artist, laid upon the major premise, rocks the foundations of the world; and he himself can indulge in this perilous occupation only because his mansion is not in the world but in the eternal heavens.

The artist's knowledge of his own creative nature is often unconscious; he pursues his mysterious way of life in a strange innocence. If he were consciously to pluck out the heart of his mystery, he might say something like this:

I find in myself a certain pattern which I acknowledge as the law of my true nature, and which corresponds to experience in such a manner that, while my behavior conforms to the pattern, I can interpret experience in power. I find, further, that the same pattern inheres in my work as in myself; and I also find that theologians attribute to God Himself precisely that pattern of being which I find in my work and in me.

I am inclined to believe, therefore, that this pattern directly corresponds to the actual structure of the living universe, and that it exists in other men as well as in myself; and I conclude that, if other men feel themselves to be powerless in the universe and at odds with it, it is because the pattern of their lives and works has become distorted and no longer corresponds to the universal pattern—because they are, in short, running counter to the law of their nature.

I am confirmed in this belief by the fact that, so far as I conform to the pattern of human society, I feel myself also to be powerless and at odds with the universe; while so far as I conform to the pattern of my true nature, I am at odds with human society, and it with me. If I am

right in thinking that human society is out of harmony
with the law of its proper nature, then my experience
again corroborates that of the theologians, who have also
perceived this fundamental dislocation in man.

If you ask me what is this pattern which I recognize
as the true law of my nature, I can suggest only that it
is the pattern of the creative mind—an eternal Idea,
manifested in material form by an unresting Energy,
with an outpouring of Power that at once inspires,
judges, and communicates the work; all these three being one and the same in the mind and one and the same
in the work. And this, I observe, is the pattern laid
down by the theologians as the pattern of the being of
God.

If all this is true, then the mind of the maker and the
Mind of the Maker are formed on the same pattern, and
all their works are made in their own image.

It is not at all likely that, if you caught the first artist
you saw passing and questioned him, he would explain
himself in these terms. He is no more accustomed than
the rest of us to look for any connection between theology and experience. Nor, as I said at the beginning, do
the theologians of today take much trouble to expound
their doctrine by way of the human maker's analogy.
They are ready to use the "Father-symbol" to illustrate
the likeness and familiarity between God and His children. But the "Creator-symbol" is used, if at all, to illustrate the deep gulf between God and His creatures.
Yet, as Berdyaev says, "The image of the artist and the
poet is imprinted more clearly on his works than on his
children." Particularly when it comes to the Trinity of

the Godhead, the emphasis is always placed on the mystery and uniqueness of the structure—as though it were a kind of blasphemy to recognize with Augustine that this, at least, is to man a homely and intimate thing, "familiar as his garter."

The disastrous and widening cleavage between the Church and the Arts on the one hand and between the State and the Arts on the other leaves the common man with the impression that the artist is something of little account, either in this world or the next; and this has had a bad effect on the artist, since it has left him in a curious spiritual isolation. Yet with all his faults, he remains the person who can throw most light on that "creative attitude to life" to which bewildered leaders of thought are now belatedly exhorting a no less bewildered humanity.

Nor is the creative mind unpractical or aloof from that of the common man. The notion that the artist is a vague, dreamy creature living in retreat from the facts of life is a false one—fostered, as I shrewdly suspect, by those to whose interest it is to keep administrative machinery moving regardless of the end-product. At the irruption of the artist into a State department, officialdom stands aghast, not relishing the ruthless realism which goes directly to essentials. It is for the sacrilegious hand laid on the major premise that the artist is crucified by tyrannies and quietly smothered by bureaucracies.[9]

[9] "At home [in 1939], the Foreign Office whole-heartedly shared the general view of Whitehall that the war was to be one of officials, by officials, for officials. In the previous conflict [1914-1918] many outsiders—mere intellectuals and journalists—had been introduced into the administrative machine. No doubt they had contributed materially to the winning of the war, but they had been a con-

As for the common man, the artist is nearer to him than the man of any other calling, since his vocation is precisely to express the highest common factor of humanity—that image of the Creator which distinguishes the man from the beast. If the common man is to enjoy the divinity of his humanity, he can come to it only in virtue and right of his making.

The wisdom of a learned man cometh by opportunity of leisure and he that hath little business shall become wise.

How can he get wisdom that holdeth the plough, and that glorieth in the goad, that driveth oxen, and is occupied in their labours, and whose talk is of bullocks?

He giveth his mind to make furrows; and is diligent to give the kine fodder.

So every carpenter and workmaster, that laboureth night and day; and they that cut and grave seals, and are diligent to make great variety, and give themselves to counterfeit imagery, and watch to finish a work:

The smith also sitting by the anvil, and considering the iron work, the vapour of the fire wasteth his flesh, and he fighteth with the heat of the furnace: the noise of the hammer and the anvil is ever in his ears, and his eyes look still upon the pattern of the thing that he maketh; he setteth his mind to finish his work, and watcheth to polish it perfectly:

So doth the potter sitting at his work, and turning the wheel about with his feet, who is alway carefully set at his work, and maketh all his work by number;

He fashioneth the clay with his arm and boweth down its strength before his feet; he applieth himself to lead it over; and he is diligent to make clean the furnace:

founded nuisance with their unconventional ideas. This must not be allowed to happen again, and, as we have seen, the 'closed shop' became the order of the day. To this initial blunder all subsequent mistakes were due, and these in their turn contributed materially to the disasters of the following spring and summer."—Sir Charles Petrie: *Twenty Years' Armistice and After.*

All these trust to their hands: and every one is wise in his work.

Without these cannot a city be inhabited: and they shall not dwell where they will, nor go up and down:

They shall not be sought for in public counsel, nor sit high in the congregation: they shall not sit on the judges' seat, nor understand the sentence of judgment; they cannot declare justice and judgment; and they shall not be found where parables are spoken.

But they will maintain the state of the world, and all their desire is in the work of their craft.[10]

[10] Ecclesiasticus xxxviii. 24-34.

POSTSCRIPT

THE WORTH OF THE WORK

IT will be seen how this matter of the worth of the work affects the inter-connected "problems" of industrialization and unemployment. Socialists have correctly observed that "an industrialized nation is a unitary nation: every part of it loses its former economic independence and virtual self-sufficiency. At the same time, if unemployment is not to be endemic, it is necessary that those new powers of production should be fully employed. That is impossible unless the products are given away." [1] They have also seen that, if the "problem" is not to be "solved" by the wholesale destruction of these products in war, it can be solved only by "distributing them among one's own citizens according to need and not according to the money-demand, and truly exchanging (as distinct from selling at a profit) the national superfluity against the superfluity of other nations." [2] So far, so good; the further conclusion is drawn that this rearrangement of social economics calls for a truly Christian love of one's neighbor. But it also calls for a no less truly Christian love of the work; and for a kind of work that shall be lovable by the Christian soul.

[1] Middleton Murry: *The Betrayal of Christ by the Churches.*
[2] Ibid.

Profit, and indeed all remuneration beyond the subsistence that enables a man to go on working, is desired because it offers an escape from work into activities more congenial and more generally admired. If the service of the machines remains hateful, men will not serve them for love; so that if the hope of escape no longer offers an inducement to work, the machines will stop, and the former conditions recur, by the inevitable dialectics of their nature. Nor will a Christian love of humanity be encouraged by the multiplication of products whose effect upon the human mind is to debase and pervert it.[3] We cannot deal with industrialism or unemployment unless we lift work out of the economic, political and social spheres and consider it also in terms of the work's worth and the love of the work, as being in itself a sacrament and manifestation of man's creative energy.

The attitude of the artist to this question is instructive. It is true that he, like everybody else, derives remuneration from his work (though not, strictly speaking, profit in the financial sense of the word, since what he invests in his work is not money but time and skill, whose returns cannot be calculated in percentages). The remuneration is frequently beyond the amount necessary to enable him to go on working. What is remarkable about him is the way in which he commonly employs the escape-from-work which the extra remuneration allows him. If he is genuinely an artist, you will find him using his escape-from-work in order to do what he calls "my own work," and nine times out of ten, this

[3] This is why the fully industrialized socialist state must resort to forced labor to keep the machines at work.

means *the same work* (i.e., the exercise of his art) *that he does for money*. The peculiar charm of his escape is that he is relieved, not from the work but from the money. His holidays are all busman's holidays. What distinguishes him here from the man who works to live is, I think, his desire to see the fulfillment of the work. Whether it is possible for a machine-worker to feel creatively about his routine job I do not know; but I suspect that it is, provided and so long as the worker eagerly desires that before all things else the work shall be done. What else causes the armaments worker to labor passionately when he knows that the existence of his country is threatened, but that his heart travels along the endless band with the machine parts and that his imagination beholds the fulfillment of the work in terms, not of money, but of the blazing gun itself, charged with his love and fear. As the author of *Ecclesiasticus* says, he "watches to finish the work"; for once, that is, he sees the end-product of his toil exactly as the artist always sees it, in a vision of Idea, Energy, and Power. It is unfortunate that so little effort should be made by Church or State to show him the works of peace in the same terms. Is the man, for example, engaged in the mass-production of lavatory cisterns encouraged to bring to his daily monotonous toil the vision splendid of an increasingly hygienic world? I doubt it; yet there is much merit in sanitary plumbing—more, if you come to think of it, than there is in warfare. But if the common man were really to adopt this high-minded and Christian attitude to the worth of his work and the needs of his neighbor, are there not some products which he would refuse at all costs to produce? I think there are; and that many of the machines would stop, unless the art of propagandist deception were carried to even greater lengths than it is at present. And who would issue the propaganda, if profit were no longer a motive? Perhaps some state which, not having enough useful commodities to exchange for necessaries, was obliged to specialize in the export of trash. And if nobody would accept the trash? In that case, we could scrap a very great number of the machines, and the "problem" of industrialization would assume a different aspect; because, in that case, every man in the world would have become an artist after his fashion.

That the artist's attitude to work is quite alien to that of the common-or-business man is a fact generally recognized and (the world being what it is) universally exploited. For example: in times of national crisis and economic stringency the writer is often requested by his publisher to accept a reduced royalty on his forthcoming book (particularly if his "message" is held to be of value to the nation), on the ground of "the increased cost of printing." The assumption is that, such is his eagerness to see his work published, he will readily cut his remuneration to the starvation line rather than deprive the world of the fruit of his toil. But it is never suggested to the printer that he should have his wages reduced on account of the educational value of the book he is printing. On the contrary, his wage is increased at the writer's expense, though the increased cost of living affects them both alike. Everybody takes this for granted. It would be irrational to suppose that this is because the printer's work is more valuable to the community than the writer's, since if all the writers stopped writing, the printers would have nothing to print, and their skill would automatically become valueless. The true reason is that the writer is known to live by a set of values which are not purely economic: he beholds the end of the work. As a common-or-business man, he requires payment for his work and is often pretty stiff in his demands; but as an artist, he retains so much of the image of God that he is in love with his creation for its own sake.

So too, the artist has two meanings for the concept of property. When he says, "This is my top-hat, my bath-room, my motor-car," he means merely that he possesses these things; but when he says, "this is my work," he means that, no matter who now possesses it, he made it. The Communist makes it a great point that the worker should own the tools of his trade; but few people in a machine age think much whether it matters that a man should feel the accomplished work to be his own. Yet this is what underlies the delight of a man in his work. True, it is not for every man—not even for every artist—to say of a work: "This is all mine, from the first conception in the brain to the last detail made with hands." The novelist may say it if he disregards the work of printer and binder; the maker of a gem-ring may say it if he disregards the work of the miner; but the playwright may not say it, nor the actor, still less the stonemason who carves the capitals for a great cathedral; yet all of them in some degree may say it if they look to the end of the work. "The ring is mine, though I may not wear it," "the Cathedral is ours, though we no more possess it than the humblest of all who worship in it." But what of the factory hand, endlessly pushing a pin into a slot? How clearly does he feel of the far-off end-product of his task, "this thing is mine"? And if he does feel proprietorship in it, how often does the contemplation afford food for the soul?

This "problem" of unemployment admits of no simple solution. As someone has truly observed, "there is no unemployment in Dartmoor Prison"—nor, indeed, is there any "problem" of the insecurity of the means of livelihood or of an over-mechanized industry. In hardness of condition and lack of liberty there is little to choose between Dartmoor and a Trappist monastery, and the looker-on might readily suppose that in both the "problem of work" had been "solved" in the same way. "Poverty, obedience, chastity" is the rule of life in both; and the convict might appear to have the advantage, since he is far likelier than the monk to return to the world some day and in the meantime enjoys a good deal more freedom of speech. Yet between the employed and the employed, between the secure and the secure, between the bound and the bound there is a difference too great to be seen in the schedules of employment.

So, too, between the worker and the worker, between the insecure and the insecure. No one is more insecure than the creative artist; in daring to dedicate himself to his work, he takes his life in his hands. If a writer loses his health or his market, he cannot look to national insurance to help him out; the cash value of his commodity is subject to every wind and whim of the public fancy; if he works slowly or badly, he has no trade-union to insure that he shall be paid at the same rate as better workers, nor, if his publisher suddenly decides to have done with him can he bring a summons against him for wrongful dismissal. He is treated with ferocious injustice by the Treasury: for if he spends six years in writing a book and at the end of the time receives a payment representing an advance on the next two years' sales, that sum which represents eight years' earnings is taxed as one year's income. Generally speaking, in fact, he is treated by the State as though he were an enemy and a parasite. And if he has not a trade-union of his own, is it not his own fault? It is; but the trade-union is intolerable in his eyes, because it might prevent him from working as fast and as well and as many hours a day as he can. The trade-union is conceived in terms of employment and not in terms of the end of the work, so that the artist's adherence to it can never be wholehearted.

It is not, of course, only the artist who thus lives dangerously out of regard for the integrity of his work. "There are not a few good farmers," says Viscount Lymington, "who have gone bankrupt for the sake of the land rather than farm badly." [4] Wherever such an attitude is found, there is the artist's way of life. Yet the integrity of the work—the stipulation that it shall be both worth doing and well done—rarely figures in any scheme for an ordered society, whether issued by Labor or by Capital. [5]

If anyone is found to insist on the integrity of the work, he is usually countered by a plausible argument:

[4] Art. in *Sunday Times*, 1.12.40.

[5] It is, however, only right to add that the leaders of the Churches in Britain have, in their Manifesto of 21 December 1940, distinguished themselves by incorporating among their additions to the Pope's "Five Points" the following pronouncement:

that all the works of men are subordinate to the needs of humanity, and that the artist's devotion to the work is devotion to a kind of abstraction—a luxury which merits consideration only after human needs have been met. If, as I maintain, the activity of creation is a primary human need, the argument answers itself. What, in any case, is a human need? It is not necessarily the same thing as a public demand. If a universal kindliness (which is what most people mean by the love of one's neighbor) is to set up the satisfaction of public demand as the worker's only goal, then the work will proceed from corruption to corruption—unless public demand can be made identical with the human need for a divine perfection in work. But this is to argue in a circle, since this identification cannot take place unless all men are made so far artists as to desire the integrity of the work.

Here we come up against the deep gulf fixed between love and kindness. "There is kindness in Love: but Love and kindness are not coterminous, and when kindness . . . is separated from the other elements of Love, it involves a certain fundamental indifference to its object, and even something like contempt of it. . . . Kindness, merely as such, cares not whether its object becomes good or bad, provided only that it escapes suffering. . . . It is for people whom we care nothing about that we demand happiness on any terms: with our

The sense of a Divine vocation must be restored to man's daily work.

This is offered as one of the "five standards by which economic situations and proposals may be tested." The signatories to this Manifesto are the Roman Catholic Archbishop of Westminster, the Anglican Archbishops of Canterbury and York, and the Moderator of the Free Church Federal Council.

friends, our lovers, our children, we are exacting and would rather see them suffer much than be happy in contemptible and estranging modes." [6]

The sterner side of love is, as we have seen,[7] powerfully present in the artist's attitude to his work; and it is equally present in the attitude of the lovers of mankind. It is a short and sordid view of life that will do injury to the work in the kind hope of satisfying a public demand; for the seed of corruption introduced into the work will take root in those who receive it, and in due season bring forth its fearful harvest.

That the eyes of all workers should behold the integrity of the work is the sole means to make that work good in itself and so good for mankind. This is only another way of saying that the work must be measured by the standard of eternity; or that it must be done for God first and foremost; or that the Energy must faithfully manifest forth the Idea; or, theologically, that the Son does the will of the Father.

[6] C. S. Lewis: *The Problem of Pain.*
[7] Chapter IX.

APPENDIX
(for handy reference)

The relevant portions of the Apostles' Creed, the Nicene Creed, and the Athanasian Creed.

1. *The Apostles' Creed*

I believe in God the Father Almighty, Maker of Heaven and earth;

And in Jesus Christ his only Son our Lord, who was conceived by the Holy Ghost;

I believe in the Holy Ghost.

2. *The Nicene Creed*

I believe in one God the Father Almighty, Maker of Heaven and earth and of all things visible and invisible;

And in one Lord Jesus Christ, the only-begotten Son of God, begotten of his Father before all worlds,

God of God, Light of Light, Very God of Very God, begotten not made, being of one substance with the Father;

By whom all things were made;

Who came down from Heaven and was incarnate by the Holy Ghost and was made man.

And I believe in the Holy Ghost the Lord, the Giver of life, who proceedeth from the Father and the Son,

Who with the Father and the Son together is worshipped and glorified;

Who spake by the prophets.

3. *The Athanasian Creed, Called also the Quicunque Vult*

The Catholic Faith is this: that we worship one God in Trinity, and Trinity in Unity, neither confounding the Persons nor dividing the Substance.

For there is one Person of the Father, another of the Son, and another of the Holy Ghost; but the Godhead of the Father, of the Son, and of the Holy Ghost is all one—the glory equal, the majesty co-eternal.

Such as the Father is, such is the Son and such is the Holy Ghost: the Father uncreate, the Son uncreate, and the Holy Ghost uncreate; the Father incomprehensible, the Son incomprehensible, and the Holy Ghost incomprehensible; the Father eternal, the Son eternal, and the Holy Ghost eternal;

And yet they are not three eternals, but one eternal; as also there are not three incomprehensibles nor three uncreated, but one uncreated and one incomprehensible.

So likewise the Father is almighty, the Son almighty, and the Holy Ghost almighty; and yet they are not three Almighties but one almighty. So the Father is God, the Son is God, and the Holy Ghost is God; and yet they are not three Gods but one God; so likewise the Father is Lord, the Son Lord, and the Holy Ghost Lord; and yet not three Lords but one Lord.

For like as we are compelled by the Christian verity to acknowledge every Person by himself to be God and Lord, so are we forbidden by the Catholic religion to say, there be three Gods or three Lords.

The Father is made of none, neither created nor begotten;

The Son is of the Father alone, neither made nor created, but begotten;

The Holy Ghost is of the Father and of the Son, neither made nor created nor begotten, but proceeding;

So there is one Father, not three Fathers; one Son, not three Sons; one Holy Ghost, not three Holy Ghosts.

And in this Trinity none is afore or after other, none is greater or less than another; but the whole three Persons are co-eternal together and co-equal.

He therefore that will be saved must thus think of the Trinity.

Furthermore, it is necessary to everlasting salvation that he also believe rightly the Incarnation of our Lord Jesus Christ. For the right faith is, that we believe and confess that our Lord Jesus Christ, the Son of God, is God and Man:

God, of the Substance of his Father, begotten before the worlds; and Man, of the Substance of his Mother, born in the world. Perfect God, and perfect Man of a reasonable soul and human flesh subsisting; equal to the Father as touching his Godhead and inferior to the Father as touching his Manhood. Who although he be God and Man, yet he is not two, but one Christ.